California Schemin'

California Schemin'

The Black Woman's Guide to Surviving in LA

Nicole D. Sconiers

Writers Club Press
San Jose New York Lincoln Shanghai

California Schemin'
The Black Woman's Guide to Surviving in LA

Writers Club Press
an imprint of iUniverse.com, Inc.

For information address:
iUniverse.com, Inc.
5220 S 16th, Ste. 200
Lincoln, NE 68512
www.iuniverse.com

ISBN: 0-595-16788-8

Printed in the United States of America

Dedication

This book is dedicated to the Dysfunctional Diva in all of us:

Stay up!

A special thanks to Lola Sconiers. Mom, you had no clue what your crazy daughter was getting into when she quit her job, sold her furniture and hopped a Greyhound bus cross country to La La Land, but you still believed and supported me. As you are so fond of saying, "You've come from a mighty long way!!!!" I love you.

Other ladies who've helped me stay in the race: Dorothy Wilder, Mary Shannon, Bumni Moore, Kenya Conway, Toinetta Jones, Dr. Paula Rankin, Dr. Margaret Simmons, Keyneica Goins, Carol King, Kim Rogers Brooks, Kim Nelson, Esther Couser, Nicole H. Williams, Jill Yesko, Yvonne Nisby, Farah Eshetu, Hyuna Ayazi, Donna Murray, Belinda Bass, Jean Wheeler, Lydia Alvarado, Ralene Banks, Yolanda Williams, G.R. Fuller, Kita Williams and Dalila Akilah Frazier.

Epigraph

I love
Sipping smoothies on Sunset
Watching the sun rise
Through smog-filled skies
Wearing open-toed shoes
In winter weather
While folks on the Right Coast
Are still draped in leather
Coats & gloves
I love
That my waitress
Doesn't bat an eye
When I order veggie tacos
& Homefries
For breakfast
And the trendy necklace I wear
Gets snagged in
The extra tracks of hair
I've acquired for the evening
But weaving our way through La La Life
Is a process for many sisters
Who still seek limelight
Even though the heat has blistered
Many a dream
Melrose mommies
Singing Crenshaw cuties' blues
With pierced tongues

We all wear tattoos
But some
Are on the inside
I love the Hollywood sign
Just out of reach
In an oasis of palm trees
And gilded stars
Planted in the concrete
I love
VIP invites
That expire at midnight
And platinum cards
That leave shards of hope
Hanging on velvet ropes
Tomorrow
No one may remember my name
But I still love LA's
Fleeting ghetto fame

"Left Coast Love"
—Nicole Sconiers © 2000

Introduction

I HAVE A SCHEME!

"Pick your enemies carefully or you'll never make it in Los Angeles."

—Rona Barrett

LA. Home of starlets, smog and silicone. Memorialized in gangsta rap lyrics and riot manuals. Clive James once called this city "paradise with a lobotomy," and I was soon to discover how the black woman fit into the scheme of things.

When I first hopped off the Greyhound bus from Norristown, PA (with an 18-month layover in San Diego), nothing could contain my eagerness at finally arriving in La La Land. Stardust coated my eyes, gilding the smoggy air and grimy streets. The unfamiliar rapid-fire Spanish resounded in my ears like a complex sonata, and I was so busy taking pictures of palm trees that I forgot to be on guard for the gangbangers and routine drivebys I had seen in 'hood movies and heard about on the nightly news.

Despite my yokel demeanor, I was more than just another small-town girl with big-time aspirations. I was a D.I.T., a Diva In Training, and ultra-confident that there was a blank star on the Hollywood Walk of Fame just waiting for my name to be engraved in it.

Growing up, it had been drilled into my brain that all a girl really needs to succeed in life is talent and determination. Having a healthy dose of both, I hit the pavement with my screenplay and a smile, trying to make my mark on Tinsel Town. As a college grad with good upbringing (only slightly dysfunctional) and a few bylines to my credit, I knew that the doors to success were wide open, waiting for me to sashay through them. But none of these attributes prepared me for the jungle that is LA.

The real power brokers in this city are dream hustlers. They know that they represent the success you strive for and they want to see how high you'll jump to attain it. I've sat in the office of a white agent I was more talented than and listened as she questioned whether or not my screenplays were "black" enough for Hollywood. At a one-on-one meeting with the CFO of an entertainment company, I watched in disbelief as the man turned on the CD player in the conference room where we were sitting and proceeded to bump and grind in front of me. Taken seriously in LA as an intelligent sister? I think not.

The black woman in Los Angeles is an anomaly. Two years of living in this city have shown me that in order to be successful in the industry we need more than talent and determination. We need looks, connections, a hefty bra size and a willingness to give it up on the legendary casting couch (with men and women). Being forty pounds overweight at the time and far from having star quality, I realized that none of those options was available nor acceptable to me. To further hinder my chances of success, I developed a debilitating chronic illness that kept me housebound for the first three months of my stay in this city. I didn't have any friends, and my wardrobe consisted mainly of muu muu's and other un-LA Fabulous items of clothing. I knew I would have to devise other means of surviving on the Left Coast.

Even if you're not an industry wannabe, day-to-day living in Los Angeles can leave you in a perpetual state of psychological road rage. This city is not conducive to the emotional well being of the black woman. Unless she is a Halle Berry lookalike, she is bypassed daily at bus stops, ignored at cash registers and shunned on the streets—a modern-day invisible woman. On one such occasion, I was perusing the aisles of a bookstore and I approached the blond clerk who was on her knees re-stocking magazines. Barely glancing up at me, she pointed to the book rack and said "We're all out of *Jet* and *Ebony* but *Essence* is on the bottom shelf." Her impertinence, which I came to discover as common in this city, wouldn't allow me to unhinge my lips to say I was actually looking for *Writer's Digest*. I just turned around and left the store.

If this city is not ignoring a sister outright, it's sending subliminal signals that she needs a cultural makeover. Fashion billboards glare down at her, daring her to aspire to Melrose's standard of beauty. If she does possess such lofty expectations, she'd better have a fierce weave and anorexic inclinations to go along with them. Back in Pennsylvania, a sister who was thick like me could feel comfortable flaunting her 5'5", 175 pound frame around. But in LA? I felt like the posterchild for liposuction. Countless newspaper ads for breast augmentation and commercials for cosmetic surgery sent daily reminders that my bodily dimensions were so uncute.

This city can be a smiling stranger…with an UZI concealed behind its back. I have even found myself dodging mental bullets from other black women. Even though I understand this "friendly fire," it still saddens me that sisters in LA are so mistrustful of one another. When we meet in the street, we barely speak. It's as if we fear the acknowledgement will make us seem weak somehow. Hailing from a small town where folks greeted each other as they went about their daily travels, I saw nothing wrong with speaking to everyone as I passed. I learned quickly enough, however, that friendly people are regarded as country bumpkins and easy to get over on in LA.

When a sister's self-preservation is threatened by external factors, she has to become as wily and cunning as B'rer Rabbit of old Negro folklore to stay alive. And success is the proverbial briar patch. She has to employ her own wits and ingenuity to stay ahead of the game or she'll be forced to hop the next Greyhound bus back to whatever small, dusty hamlet she left behind. I was willing to face a slow death rather than return to Norristown empty handed (meaning without achieving the stardom I knew I was destined for). Drawing on strength and self-confidence I didn't even know I possessed, I was at least willing to salsa with the dream hustlers in LA. And when I discovered that I didn't know all the right dance moves, I improvised as I went along.

One thing you can be sure of: dream chasing in this city is a revolving door. Friends who are prettier, more talented and better connected that I am have come and gone, most times returning to their hometowns emotionally beat down. I was not supposed to be the one left standing: a fat, small-town girl with a housewife's wardrobe, chronic asthma and no access to the Hollywood players. I've suffered some scars myself along the way, to be sure, but my collective experiences have helped mold me into a fearless fly girl!

Girls, try this at home! This book is written for my fellow sirens in the struggle, whether you have relocated here to make it in the industry, or are surviving through a summer's visit with your cousin Rasheeda on Crenshaw. Now it can be told. I offer these observations as testament to my own hand-to-hand combat in the conference rooms, clubs and streets of LA. Black women can survive in this city without becoming…

CHAPTER 1
DYSFUNCTIONAL DIVAS

---

*"We black women are the single group in the
West intact. And anybody can see we're pretty
shaky..."*

—Nikki Giovanni

MUCH can be learned about a city by its inhabitants, so it was no shock
to discover that LA is home to many Dysfunctional Divas.

You might spot her on the dance floor of the club, funking up a Donna
Karan cocktail dress (pricetag still tucked inside), which she will surely
return to the department store the following day. Or she may saunter
straight into the church sanctuary from the after party, clutching a Bible
to skin still spangled with glitter.

I have crossed paths with many divas in my daily excursions. I call them
dysfunctional because they have all the material trappings of a prima
donna without her sense of propriety.

Most of the D.D.'s I see traipsing along the streets of Los Angeles are
bred not born. Living in this city can make a sister lose her mind! Hence
the would-be starlet riding around in a leased convertible BMW and
sleeping on a futon. She's trying to live like a leading lady instead of a leas-
ing one. Now she knows her mama didn't bring her up like that, but LA
living can make even the most ingrained hometraining fly right out the
window.

Because Black women in this city are so used to being dissed in department stores, pushed aside at cosmetic counters and patronized in board meetings, most of us are starved for attention.

> ### You Might Be a Dysfunctional Diva If...
>
> 1. You rock Versace, but can't spell it.
> 2. You have a Landcruiser *and* a landlord.
> 3. You're always late with the rent, but never late for a hair appointment.
> 4. You use a flyer from the club as a bookmark in your Bible.
> 5. You call your agent more than your mother.

When I first relocated to LA, I exhibited D.D. tendencies. Appearance is everything, and I was reminded again and again that "the important people see you coming." I tried to mold myself into the image of someone who had it together. I leased a brand new SUV I could not afford (much less keep gas in), acquired five more inches of hair and went on a strict vegetarian diet to shed forty pounds in three months. These actions would have been cause for a visit to the therapist had I been living on the East Coast, but in LA traits such as these are not only tolerated but encouraged.

Something in the air out here makes us irrational. As soon as we step off the plane, train or automobile that brought us to LA, we feel the need to be seen...by any means necessary! Friends who visit me from the East Coast blow a month's rent on a new wardrobe to rock on their sojourn in Cali and seriously contemplate name changes.

One Dysfunctional Diva I know, another product of a small town, was trying to make a name for herself in LA as a professional flunky. She would befriend people in the industry, then follow them around like a homeless puppy scrounging for scraps.

I admit, I was *slightly* star struck when I first got to town. I carried a disposable camera around in my purse and frequented all the star-friendly hangouts just to get my gaze on. But the common sight of celebrities picking up their clothes from the cleaners or carrying grocery bags from Ralphs supermarket can be a demystifying experience. Not for my friend, however. Her conversations were peppered with the names of entertainers whose video sets she had visited or whose parties she had attended. And her photo album? You would have thought she was a member of the paparazzi! This fawning fly girl had more pictures of herself hugged up with famous people than with her own family members. Since she was never able to taste fame for herself, she wanted desperately to live vicariously through these celebrities. Homegirl could hear the music, but she couldn't get into the club.

I often wondered why these "friends" never kicked her down with a job. The menial tasks that they delegated to her (dropping off scripts, picking up dry cleaning) were nothing more than the standard duties of your garden-variety personal assistant. Yet, to hear this diva tell it, she was on par with the stars. I once asked her why she felt the need to forever follow after famous folks. "If you want filet mignon, you don't go to a Mexican restaurant," was her smug retort.

Tragically, she was too busy following in the platinum-plated footsteps of others to realize her own true talent. Being a flunky may be fine for some, but photo ops don't pay the bills. When she was unable to sustain herself in LA, my friend had to move back to Smallsville, U.S.A. with her parents. The last I heard, she had been committed to a mental institution for threatening her mom with a butter knife. I wonder if her "friends" out here even know or care about her condition. One thing's for sure: they don't serve filet mignon at the state hospital.

Another D.D. I know was featured on the cover of a popular magazine for black men and could run circles around Cindy Crawford on the catwalk. Homegirl is flawless! Unlike other catty cover girls I had encountered, she was down-to-earth and had a head for business. She was a model's model, if you will. Women in LA know about hustling, which I'll deal with further in a later chapter. Every time I saw this caramel cutie, she was working on a new proposal or business plan or flyer to promote herself and her event coordinating business. I have to hand it to her; she never gave up. This sister managed to reinvent herself more than Madonna and her tenacity gave me the courage to believe I, too, could survive and be successful in La La Land.

My running buddy had all the accoutrements of a Hollywood diva: a fabulous wardrobe, an extensive Rolodex of industry folks and attitude for days. Unfortunately, she was never able to translate that into material success. Business venture after business venture evaporated and her modeling gigs were barely paying the rent. To make matters worse, she adamantly refused to get a day job.

It seems a little dysfunctional that my friend chose not to get a nine-to-five until one of her side gigs paid off. In the two years that I've been acquainted with her, I've never known her to hold down a regular job. This sister has been on more interviews than Janet Jackson, but never once worked anywhere for more than a week or two.

The final straw came when she was forced to move out of her apartment, two steps ahead of the sheriff escorting her and her property out. Her belongings were divided between her storage unit and friends' homes. At the time of this writing, she still has a few items of clothing hanging in my hallway closet.

When I saw my friend last, she looked tired and defeated. Her caramel skin, which used to shine so luxuriously, looked like dried out fudge. The downfall of this former cover girl really saddened and frightened me. If she couldn't make it in LA, how could I expect to be survive when I didn't possess half the attributes or connections that she did?

The aforementioned situations may seem extreme to some unaware readers, but scenarios like these are as common in LA as road rage on the 405 Freeway. Sometimes we black women start believing our own press releases. We get so caught up in the rush of "making it" that we assume we are invincible. Only when the sheriff or the repo man comes knocking do we realize we are not.

I was talking to Gabrielle Union (the actress who has the distinction of making history as the first black co-star on the sitcom "Friends") about how black women can survive in LA without becoming institutionalized. Like me, the outspoken Union grew up in a small-town and experienced culture shock upon relocation to La La Land.

"You can't come out here thinking 'I was homecoming queen in Tuscaloosa, Alabama, so I'm about to be the next Halle Berry,'" jokes the flawless actress. "It's best to be multi-dimensional. Have other interests besides this industry. I have a degree from UCLA, so I don't have the same kind of desperate anxiety with auditions. I'm computer literate. I know Word. I can get a job," she laughs. "If you're not working, go back to school. Get teaching credentials. It's just about being practical and using common sense. Don't spend all of your money on a Versace outfit and you haven't paid your DWP bill."

It doesn't help that LA encourages such off-the-wall behavior. This city is, for most people, the fabled fountain of youth. Young (and not-so-young) industry hopefuls flock here by the busload trying to get their party on and make a quick buck. They learn soon enough that LA has reneged on more than a few economic promises.

There is no such thing as age-appropriate behavior in La La Land. I know actresses pushing 40 who club every weekend with the twentysomething crowd. One woman at least my mother's age came up to me at a listening party and asked me if I was feeling Jay-Z's latest song. She knew more about Hip Hop culture than I did! Some sisters in LA hold onto their carefree childhood a lot longer than their East Coast counterparts. One of the pitfalls of holding age at bay is putting off responsibilities. Hence the 28-year-old who is working part-time, living with her parents, but driving around in a Landcruiser. Or the 35-year-old who can't pay her rent on time, but just has to have that bomb $800 Chanel purse. It all goes back to my earlier theory that something in the air out here makes a sister forfeit her common sense. By any means necessary.

There's nothing wrong with being a ghetto superstar (exhibiting such flair will go a long way in getting you noticed in LA). A delicate balance must be maintained, however. I'm still struggling to hold on to my equilibrium, but one of the ways I've gotten attention is by having...

CHAPTER 2
ONE SUPERFICIAL
GIRLFRIEND

NO DIVA should be without an S.G. This chick has panache, but can't pronounce it, a fierce wardrobe and access to all the guest lists in town. A true vixen, she can tell you the hangouts to meet industry people, give you the rundown on Hollywood relationships and recommend a good day spa.

I lucked up by latching onto one of these shallow sirens at the club. She was propped in a corner, drink in hand, surveying the urban landscape. Homegirl was dressed pretty casually for an LA soiree—jeans and a tank top—but she far outshined the other hoochie-clad mommies in the room. This sister was so fierce, the only thing missing was her theme music. The brothers were flocking to her. Even I was feeling her energy and I inched along the wall toward her to find out her "secret."

I overheard this dimepiece telling an admirer that she was a writer. Green light! I immediately set out to network with her. Now since LA is a city much given to same-sex couplings, I didn't want my future S.G. to think I was trying to get with her. I enlisted the aid of a male hanger on at the bar to introduce us. After some small talk, he asked for her card. She handed him a laminated number bearing her headshot, which she produced from the cutest little leopard-skinned business card holder. I introduced myself as a writer as well (although I had just enrolled in a UCLA screenwriting program and had yet to complete a real script). We made plans to "do lunch" the following week and it was on and popping!

Now a true Superficial Girlfriend will try to enhance your image. Because she has a reputation for looking good, it behooves her to surround herself with friends who turn heads as well. These girls can be blunt, but all for the sake of beauty. On our initial lunch date, this high-classed hottie told me that blazers were to be worn in the office, not at the club. In other words, my wardrobe was too frumpy and the colors I wore were too drab. How could I explain to her, a perfect size six, that the purpose of my bulky clothes was to play down my 175 pound frame? Halters and baby tee-shirts might be fine for women who attend Tae-bo classes on the regular, but I dared not reveal my thick arms to the world for fear I would be mistaken for a Sumo wrestler. My newfound friend scoffed at this idea. She convinced me that with a more colorful, trendier wardrobe, people would pay attention to my style, not my girth.

After lunch, we went shopping at the Beverly Center for more fly-girl friendly apparel. She immediately began incorporating pastels into my colorless world. I discovered that powder blue didn't go out with 70s leisure suits and shocking pink had me blushing like a schoolgirl. I was also turned onto the wonderful world of thongs. Prior to this, I had been accustomed to wearing high-waisted "grandma drawers," even on days that I didn't have my period. But through my S.G. I learned that no self-respecting diva would be caught dead showing a panty line in LA. Thongs, or t-backs as she affectionately referred to them, were recommended because "the booty just sits right" in them.

After that first buying expedition, I felt like a new woman. Shopping bags in tow, I knew that me and my S.G. could conquer this town. With my brains and her looks, we would be a modern day Thelma and LaWeave, a force to be reckoned with at all the parties and pitching rooms in town.

Unfortunately, my S.G. didn't have such grand plans for our future. I was her eating-clubbing-and-shopping buddy. Period. Anytime I tried to introduce a meaningful subject into our conversations, or suggest an outing at the museum or art gallery, I was blown off. This namebrand belle didn't have time to partake in such frivolity. She had moved to LA to get her party on and to make a name for herself, the key word being "self."

> *"Most divas in LA don't have time for sisterhood. They lament the lack of down-to-earth and "real" girlfriends on the Left Coast, but once you bare your heart and try to show them that you are trustworthy, they avoid you like the repo man."*

In retrospect, I realize that my Superficial Girlfriend envisioned herself in the role of savior and I was her lowly convert. Once she had succeeded in my style redemption, it was time for her to move on to the next fashion-challenged disciple.

Don't make the same mistake that I did of trying to turn an S.G. into a genuine friend. Most divas in LA don't have time for sisterhood. They lament the lack of down-to-earth and "real" girlfriends on the Left Coast, but once you bare your heart and try to show them that you are trustworthy, they avoid you like the repo man. Sad, but true. If it's real friendship you yearn for—a sisterfriend to phone at three in the morning after a crushing breakup, or someone to share your joy in finding an agent—you'd better cultivate relationships with friends from your hometown and be prepared for some outlandish long distance bills.

A few true girlfriends from the East Coast question why I waste my time maintaining counterfeit friendships. While I do have two or three homies who I trust to have my back in this city, most of the women I meet decide whether or not to befriend me on the basis of how I look and the extensiveness of my Rolodex. That's just the reality of friendship in LA. When I first relocated here, I assumed that since these sisters were also hustling to succeed in the business, our respective struggles would bond us together. How wrong I was! Making it in LA is more cutthroat than a sorority's hazing process. Since so few black women get to join that exclusive (and elusive) Hollywood insider club, each additional candidate for membership is seen as a threat to their own chances of being admitted.

I have to warn you that if you're allergic to phony people, make sure you bring plenty of tissues to LA. Some of the women I've encountered are more shallow than baby pools. When you befriend sisters at an industry party or the club, they're on a mission to see and be seen. In other words, they're fronting as well. When you smile or try to make small talk, they ain't having it, unless you have a title or connections to some Hollywood player who can advance their careers. Even though they might be new to the city and don't have many friends, they never seem to need anyone but themselves.

There are times when I wish I could just get together with some friends and watch a movie, or sit home and act silly over nothing. But for many LA women, bonding is achieved through partying. Time is of the essence out here. To them a weekend spent watching videos or playing Spades means you're sleeping on an opportunity to be successful. When your only commonality is clubbing and networking, it's hard to get in touch with a sister's real side. Three years later, you're still calling her to go out and clubhop, when you realize you don't know her middle name or her favorite color.

In the jungle that is LA, it's hard to find true camaraderie among these hustling honies. It's either exploit or be exploited in this city. If you're going to use someone, make sure she can at least raise your fashion I.Q.

In all fairness, I have to admit that I was using my S.G. pretty much in the same way she was using me—for convenience. Even after I discovered that we weren't going to be best buddies, I continued to look to her for style pointers. To this day, I still regard her as the best dresser that I have ever been acquainted with in LA.

Clothes do make the woman, but more than that, an essential concept for the Diva In Training is grasping the idea of...

CHAPTER 3
LA CHIC

THE SECRET to LA Chic is attitude. It's that laid back "Yeah, I'd still be the bomb in slippers and a torn tee-shirt" demeanor that is in itself an accessory.

Most sisters who relocate to LA are clueless about how the natives dress and often end up sticking out like a botched boob job.

When an East Coast girlfriend, who is preparing for a visit, asks what LA women are wearing, I tell her "As little as possible."

My initiation to the LA Chic concept took place at the very first industry function I was invited to. Since I was forty pounds overweight at the time, I knew I couldn't put my back fat and love handles on display. I didn't know about having Mad Confidence (*see Chapter 4*) back then, so the next best thing was to be as colorful as possible to attract attention. I donned a fire engine red ankle-length skirt, complete with a red halter, red blazer and red stilettos. This disastrous getup was topped off with ruby lipstick. Can you say ghetto vampire? I looked like the unfortunate victim of a murder scene, but you couldn't tell me I wasn't fine!

When I opened the door to let my S.G. in, I couldn't wait to see her reaction at how fast her star pupil was learning. I was finally breaking out of my dreary wardrobe. But when she raised her perfectly arched eyebrow and gave me a slight smirk, I knew I'd struck out. She was clad in a simple white halter and black pants, carrying the cutest black clutch. As I struggled down the sidewalk, feet swollen in six-inch stilettos, I enviously glanced down at my girlfriend's feet. Her size 6's were clad in a pair of funky platforms and two of her perfectly pedicured toes were adorned with silver rings.

When we arrived at the party, my S.G. attracted more than a few appreciative glances in her ensemble, even receiving a hug from my favorite soap opera stud who was on hand for the festivities. I was in awe at seeing the man up close and personal for the first time, but neglected to speak to him for fear that he would mistake me for a cherry tomato in my outfit.

The cardinal rule to remember for dressing in LA is that simple is better. Simple is sexy. And accessories do make the outfit. Hailing from a small town on the East Coast, I was used to covering up my body for three-quarters of the year, choosing only to bare some skin in the warmer months. But in LA, summertime is year round. Just stroll down Sunset in September and you'll be treated to a veritable flesh fest.

When I first started experiencing LA nightlife, I made the mistake of throwing on everything in my closet when I got dressed, the telltale sign of a neophyte LA partygoer. Now the trick is to play up a simple pair of pants and shirt with an adorable pair of earrings or a trendy necklace. That way the attitude speaks for itself.

Top 10 LA Chic Accessories

1. Basic black dress
2. Booty hugging bootleg jeans
3. A cute clutch
4. A trendy choker
5. Toe rings
6. Glimmer body dust
7. Rhinestone belt (doubles as a necklace)
8. Black strappy shoes
9. Cute halter/Baby tees
10. Invisible necklace with earrings to match

Since the sun shines almost 365 days a year in La La Land, it's not uncommon to see sisters rocking open-toed shoes and halter tops around the calendar. It's as if the illusion of an ever-present sun seems to continually warm these women. Now they may come down with croup the next day, but as long as they looked good at the industry party or the concert the night before, it's all good.

One January, some Baltimore buddies came to visit me and I took them to the club so they could see LA Chic in action. My poor partners were huddled together at the table, still trying to escape the clenches of the cool LA night air. They preferred to be smart rather than sexy, and were dressed in blazers, leather coats and boots. Their jaws dropped to see sisters sashaying into the room wearing as much material as Barbie Dolls. But hey, some women in this city have the mentality that they are going to look fabulous even if it kills them.

I initially thought that my S.G.'s skills at being a style maven were inborn. She later admitted that she was introduced to LA Chic by growing up watching Soul Train. She would scope out what the gyrating mommies on the show were wearing, then run to her local mall and try to emulate them. A lot of snazzy dressers out here probably received their fashion education the same way.

Another sister-in-style who used to live in my building also helped to raise my fashion I.Q. On a daily basis, she rocked outfits worthy of a *Vogue* centerfold, rarely wearing the same clothes twice. I wondered how this chic *chica* was able to afford such a fabulous wardrobe on her salary, which wasn't much more than I was earning. My neighbor slyly confessed that she was a "street model." Translation: she would go shopping, test her clothes out on the sidewalks of LA and then return them to the store. This vamp reminded me that all clothes came with a "money back guarantee," and she was determined to take advantage of that policy as often as possible. I'm sure a lot of pricetag tuckers are "street modeling" around LA, trying to be beautiful on a budget. My conscience, and the fact that I don't want to suffer from pricetag scars on my body, has prohibited me from going that route. But hey, it works for her. This chick is now billing herself as an image consultant and has several clients. Only in LA!

If you're fashion-challenged like I was, it helps to surround yourself with women who know how to whip up a wardrobe. Another sister who contributed to my sense of style is my dear friend from Riverside. I met her in 1995 when I visited Cali for the first time to be in a wedding. To me, she was the embodiment of LA Chic. Because this concept is mainly based on attitude, she can rock a shirt from Target and make it look like it came from Rodeo Drive. This diva is a rarity: a native-born black California girl who wears her own hair. My friend taught me some invaluable pointers, like using a dot of mascara to transform a zit into a mole and wearing white eyeliner on the eyelids to open up the eyes. She's the kind of woman with an effortless and timeless beauty that can't be purchased at the M.A.C. counter. Whenever I'm in doubt about rocking rhinestones or beads with an outfit, my friend is another style maven I can count on at all times.

Once I got down the knack of dressing LA Chic, I had to try it out on my kinfolk back on the East Coast. I flew home for a visit one summer, feeling like the black Jackie O. When I stepped off the plane wearing a simple lime green dress, lime green shoes and carrying a fabulous matching purse, Norristown wasn't ready for me. My family thought I had hit the big time (and secretly, I thought I had, too). They loved my new look! Here stood the girl who used to make such fashion faux pas as wearing pantyhose with sandals and carrying clutches that didn't match the color of her shoes. But I was fabulous, and that made up for my former style transgressions. I was an Accessorizer With Attitude.

And speaking of attitudes, another must-have accessory for the fearless woman's wardrobe is...

CHAPTER 4
MAD CONFIDENCE

"All you need in this life is ignorance and confidence, and then success is sure."

—Mark Twain

IF you want to know what Mad Confidence is check out the 250 pound sister in the nightclub rocking hip huggers and a handkerchief halter. Or peep the SAG/AFTRA card-carrying "actress" whose demo reel consists mainly of home videos and a stint on Judge Judy.

Mad Confidence is a trait as essential to a sister's survival in LA as a can of pepper spray in the purse. It's an eye-stinging concoction that will let them have it!

I must give props to my partner-in-crime who is a freelance entertainment reporter. This princess is a supreme example of Mad Confidence. Another small-town girl, she came to LA on a whim and managed to finagle a job in the industry. She was bluffing about her qualifications of course, or as she states "putting more on it," but homegirl has never failed to get her size nines in the door.

We were invited to attend a tribute to the legendary Richard Pryor one evening and girlfriend was definitely working the room. Tape recorder in hand, she approached a high-profile comedian/actor as he waited to go on stage. The man initially protested that he didn't handle his business like that, but she wangled an on-the-spot interview out of him anyway. This *chica* does not take no for an answer. Not only did she make baby boy break down and take us to a more secluded section of the VIP lounge to conduct the interview, she kept him so long, his peeps had to practically pry him away so he could do his thing on stage.

> ### *Mad Confidence Is...*
>
> 1. Hoping to find Mr. Right in LA.
> 2. Quitting your day job and then going on a shopping spree.
> 3. Knowing you'll find an agent because your script is the bomb!
> 4. Lending money to an out-of-work director who promises to repay you when his movie gets picked up.
> 5. Going to the club with no money, not being on the guestlist, but knowing you'll get in because someone once said you favored Janet Jackson.

A supermodel happened to be in the house for the festivities that evening and my girlfriend asked if she could take her picture. The glamazon practically ran away from us, claiming she would stop for the photo op after she returned from the ladies room. Well, my friend may not work the runway, but she can work a supermodel attitude. She looked the cover girl dead in the eye and told her she'd better hightail it back from the bathroom and not try to escape out the back door. In amazement, I watched as she of the mega endorsements twirled around in her tracks and consented to take the picture. Got confidence?

Shady as it seems, that's the way sisters have to scheme in this town. We can't play down our self-worth (or lack thereof) if we want to be taken seriously and respected. Even if you're not an industry wannabe, I'm still prescribing a good dose of Mad Confidence to survive in this city. Most LA denizens are certifiably crazy and you need to be able to hold your own so as not to be eaten alive.

Let me give you an example of the lunacy that occurs daily. My visiting East Coast homey was propositioned on the dance floor of a nightclub by a drunken foreigner who wanted to get busy with her in the back of his Volvo. She was also offered two hundred dollars to escort a middle-aged lawyer home as she sat eating in a diner, and was approached for initiation into the swinging lifestyle of a married couple as she sat sipping cappuccino in Starbucks. And this was all in one day! But my girlfriend played it off like she couldn't understand the foreigner's accent; she proudly explained to the lawyer that he wouldn't be able to afford her even if his last name was Cochran and told the swingers no thanks, they weren't her type. She didn't cop an attitude with the morons; all of this was relayed to them in her typical deadpan demeanor. Had homegirl not possessed the spunkiness to defend herself in these three scandalous situations, she could have fallen victim to these LA predators.

Recently, I met Tai, a college student and a transplant from New York who sums up surviving on the Left Coast like this: "LA is all about attitude. You have to be kind of 'bitchy.' On the East Coast, no one acts bitchy as a rule," she laughs, "but in LA, if you act bitchy, then you're the bomb." Tai is right in many aspects. I'm not advising sisters to go out and act like the second coming of Joan Crawford, but just know that a little extra self-assurance goes a long way.

Mad Confidence doesn't just work wonders when protecting yourself from social deviants; it goes a long way in masking low self-esteem. Like the saying goes, "Fake it 'til you make it!"

I lacked a positive sense of self-worth because I was at an all-time high of 175 pounds and going through a serious depression. Being a size 14 in La La Land, when even some size 6's are considered full-figured, is enough to make even the most resolute sister question her self-esteem. I knew I was attractive, above that I was a talented writer. I wouldn't be able to convince anyone of these attributes, however, because my girth kept me from engaging in a conversation with anyone on a professional level. Now I knew that one-legged men could sell screenplays and deaf writers could sell novels, but being fat seemed to be a fate worse that getting caught with a hole in your panties.

My modeling friend once gave me some good advice about confidence. During one of my self-pity parties, I confessed to her that I would never be able to believe in myself until I lost weight. Her next words shocked me, coming from someone who could give Tyra Banks a run for her money. My friend told me that I was beautiful just as I was. Until I was able to believe that, regardless of what the scale said, I would never feel good about myself. Through her I learned that confidence is like an aura; it radiates to your outer being and makes other people gravitate toward that light.

Because I was horizontally-challenged, I lacked not only self-assurance, but pride. My relationship with my S.G. was unraveling because I would attend industry parties with her, but refuse to network with head honchos who could help my career. I couldn't get people to look at me three ways. The low point in our friendship came when I was at a mixer with her and she became engaged in an animated discussion with my favorite soap opera sweetie. She knew how enamored I was of this man (er, I mean his acting moved me), and I stood in the shadows, hoping she would toss me a few kernels from their conversation. But did she introduce us? Nay. She turned away from the finest guy I have ever laid eyes on and stalked over to me hissing, "Why didn't you come over and talk to him?"

Being a perfect size six and an ultra diva with Mad Confidence for miles, it was never a question that hobnobbing with celebrities would come easy to my S.G. She thought it was her birthright. I was 5'5" and three sizes away from believing in myself. The thought of engaging in social intercourse with that man, or any other person of power, was for me an act of rape. They'd have to tie me down and pull a train on me to get me to utter the first syllable.

None of this did I relay to my S.G. After that night, she vowed that if I wanted to stay on her team, I had better learn to speak up, "or else." I heard the finality in her voice and it motivated and enraged me. She was threatening to excommunicate me from the temple she had erected to Divadom. Who did Miss Thing think she was? And furthermore, I had viable talent as a writer, where her only gifts lie in accessorizing and socializing. After that incident, I was determined to display Mad Confidence at any cost.

The next opportunity arose none too soon. A few months later, I was rolling solo at a launch party kicking off the soap opera stud's new website, and showcasing his new calendar. My future baby's daddy was floating across the room, buoyed by his entourage and a sea of female well wishers. As he drifted nearer to me, I did the unthinkable: I called out his name like we went way back and gave a ceremonious wave. I expected the brother to simply nod his head in acknowledgement and float on, but his next actions shocked me. His face lit up like a lantern and he held out his hands, imploring me to "show some love." I stumbled into his outstretched arms, almost needing to be held upright. I hugged him so long and so tightly, I thought I was going to have an imprint of his bulging pecs on my shirt. He asked if I was enjoying the party, while simultaneously stroking my cheek and neck. After momentarily blacking out, I came to and managed to carry on an intelligent conversation with him.

Now maybe that's the way baby boy carries on with all of his female fans. However, I'm certain that the opportunity to speak to him would have never arisen had my confidence not been bolstered by my S.G.'s remark.

In parting, this black Adonis touched my hair and I laughingly moved my head from his probing fingers. I was feeling him, but messing with a black woman's hair, especially if she has just had it done, can sometimes precipitate violence.

This brings me to another crucial topic that must be addressed: answering the age-old question...

CHAPTER 5
TO WEAVE OR NOT TO
WEAVE?

"She hath more hair than wit."
—William Shakespeare
"The Two Gentlemen of Verona"

NO BOOK on Black women in LA would be complete without dealing with the hair issue. Hair is so big out here that I'm positive the reason the city burned so long during the riots of '91 was due to the abundance of synthetic hair shops in the area.

I got my first weave when I moved to LA in 1998. Growing up on the East Coast, and hailing from a small town, it was considered taboo to wear someone else's tresses in your hair and pass them off as your own. Due in part to my fear of being ridiculed and my feminist aspirations (feminists did not wear fake hair), I shunned the notion of getting a weave.

In high school, my good girlfriend at the time threw caution to the wind and came home one day with her hair about six inches longer. I knew of no magic grease that she was using to make her hair grow, so I figured she had gotten a weave. It was wet and wavy and she sported her new growth with flair. She was the first real-live black girl I knew who wore fake hair. Although she, too, lived in an impoverished area of town, my friend was determined to be glamorous at any cost. She was considered the 'hood's answer to Marilyn Monroe. When I walked down the street with her, I felt both pride and fear. I was proud that she had the courage to rock hair that wasn't hers and make it look damned good and fearful that I would be vicariously linked to her and considered a sham as well.

Black men on the East Coast don't dig sisters wearing hair with price tags. Indeed, this practice has made weave wearers the butt of many stand up comedians' jokes.

I remember walking down South Street in nearby Philadelphia one night with my girlfriend, who at this time was sporting a sleek ponytail that fell halfway down her back. She knew she was looking good. One brother on the corner remarked as we passed by, "Yo, sis. That horse is looking for you. He wants to know if he can have his tail back." I laughed silently to myself at his joke, unaware that when I moved to LA years later, that same "horse" would be hunting for me as well.

When a good friend of mine who was coming to visit from Richmond, VA asked how LA women were wearing their hair, I replied that they weren't; they were wearing someone else's. No other city that I've visited boasts such a vast population of black women with weaves, extensions, wigs or glue-on pieces. In Philly, Atlanta, D.C., New York and Detroit, where sisters are huge on hair, it isn't out of the ordinary for a woman to add a little something extra to her own 'do for a special occasion. But in LA, sisters are treating every day like a special event.

All-Time Favorite Weave Styles I Have Sported

1. Classic Chinese bob
2. Neo jheri curl
3. Shirley Temple curlz with a ghetto twist
4. Updated upsweep
5. Wash and wear, "I got good hair!"

Call me a hypocrite, but I am allowed to criticize weaves because I have worn one. Or two. Or three. Being plain old Nicole didn't seem to cut it for me. Short of getting cosmetic surgery, I needed to do something drastic to distinguish myself in LA. Since nobody knew who I was, I could get a weave and totally revamp my whole image.

I got my first weave sewn in by a woman who boasted singers Janet Jackson and Toni Braxton as clientele. I wondered why she was doing hair out of her basement if she had such top-notch customers, but didn't have the audacity to ask her.

The woman's assistant drove with me to a store on Crenshaw where I was to pick out two packs of human hair needed for the procedure. The place was a hair emporium. Sisters, Latinas and a few white women were crowding the aisles like frenzied shoppers at Macy's on a Super Saturday. There was no shame in their game. They boldly tried on tresses in the mirror, modeling for friends as if they were contemplating buying a new coat instead of someone else's hair. One woman had a stack of tracks in front of her on the counter, with prices starting at $35 a pack. Since I was daring to be different, I convinced myself that I was going to buy chestnut locks (conveniently ignoring the fact that my real hair was jet black).

As soon as I stepped out on the sidewalk, the first twinge of guilt hit me. I was selling out. I clutched the anonymous black plastic bag to my chest, like a thief with misgivings, and slunk back to the woman's basement for my initiation into Weavedom.

To the uninitiated (which includes most white women), weaves are performed something like this: the person's real hair is braided securely in rows, or in a circle, then the weft of human hair (or synthetic hair), called a "track," is sewn into the braid. Usually most stylists will leave out some of the person's real hair and then strategically comb it back to conceal the track. This process can take anywhere from three to six hours.

My weavologist had deft fingers and the whole torturous procedure took under three hours. When she finished, I took one look in the mirror she had hanging over her washer and fell instantly and forever in love. I was a superstar! I was beautiful. I had fourteen inches of some poor Malaysian woman's hair sewn into my scalp and I was grinning like I'd just discovered the next best thing to the hot comb.

> *"I don't advocate wearing a weave and I don't advocate not wearing one. It's hard enough to make it in this city if you're on your own, and sometimes a little extra hair brings out the rebel in a sister (or at least allows her to go incognegro)."*

The two years that I wore a weave took me through a love-hate relationship with my hair. I had to convince my friends on the East Coast that I hadn't sold out, yet maintain my 'do so that I could style with my new West Coast buddies.

Black women in LA understand weaves. If they like how you wear your hair, they will come up to you and ask you if your hair is real and who styles it. On the East Coast, such impudence would be cause for a good chewing out, or even a backhand slap. But out here? That behavior is as common as body piercing. I have even found myself studying the back of some anonymous woman's head to see if I could detect the telltale tracks. I pity black women with hair that is naturally long, for in LA people will always suspect that their hair is fake. Guilty until proven weaveless. One of my buddies, whose real hair hangs to her bra strap, is constantly offended by women and men who question if her hair is real. But that was in the past. Even though her God-given hair is long enough for three or four heads, she still couldn't resist the temptation to "bulk up." Now she sports a piece in the back of her head (even though she will swear up and down that "ain't nothing fake on me"). Good luck!

As much as I loathe fake hair, I can't deny the "benefits" that come along with wearing it. People do look at you differently, as if you possess a certain inner glow that radiates to your outer self. Men open doors for you and even other women find reasons to make small talk. Once when I was stopped at a red light, two Latino brothers pulled up next to my truck. The passenger leaned out his window, commenting that he thought my hair was beautiful. I accepted the compliment with a smile thinking, "It is my hair. I got the receipt for it."

If you go out to the club in LA, you'll see that weaves are worn as an accessory. It goes without saying that you'll find more tracks at the night club than on Prince's double CD. I have personally witnessed men passing over beautiful sisters with shorter locks in favor of less attractive women with hair hanging down like a horse's mane. Their favoritism convinced me that even if a woman's grill is jacked up, a weave can compensate for her lack of looks.

When I finally decided to rid myself of the weave that I had loved/hated for two years, I was like a druggie taking my last hit. I was a track addict and taking out my fake hair definitely had me going through withdrawal symptoms. How would people who had known me as NICOLE react to knowing me as nicole? My own hair was of length, but it definitely didn't have celebrity status. It didn't flow from side to side when I moved my head and it surely wasn't the bomb accessory.

You have to have Mad Confidence in LA to sport a weave and you have to have Mad Confidence not to sport one. I choose to wear my own hair now and everyday I love my locks a little bit more. It's like reclaiming a childhood friend that you've lost touch with for all these years. It's all grown up now, but it's sassy, funky and more precious than you'd ever imagined.

I am still trying to crack the enigma of weaves. I think that doing so will help me to better understand who I am. Truth be told, my dresser drawer is filled with various tracks and pieces in case I ever feel like experimenting. Thankfully, I haven't had the urge to yet.

I know that sisters aren't the only ones who wear weaves. More than a few white women have gotten into the game (or, as I was advised by a stylist, have re-entered the sport. They were rocking falls and extensions in the early 1900s way before sisters could even afford to). One white beautician, whose home I visited, parted her hair and excitedly showed me how her hair was braided underneath and how neatly the tracks were sewn in. It's as if Rapunzel was saying, "See, we are sisters beneath the skin." Or beneath the pin, I should say.

When you look at it, it's actually silly that a hank of hair can be used to validate or invalidate a sister. I don't advocate wearing a weave and I don't advocate not wearing one. It's hard enough to make it in this city if you're on your own, and sometimes a little extra hair brings out the rebel in a sister (or at least allows her to go *incognegro*).

Speaking of rebelling, crashing parties in LA is another way of getting noticed, especially if you happen to crash…

CHAPTER 6
INDUSTRY PARTIES

"I'm so tired of these fake functions...but I'll be back next week!"

—overheard at an industry party

GROWING UP in the boondocks, the only stars we saw were through a telescope. Present in most of us was the small-town girl's dream of running away to the big city and becoming famous.

When the job fair was held at our school, we all flocked to the modeling agency booth (little did we know, they were mostly on site to humor us). We all knew we had "the look" and were just waiting for Hollywood to come to town and discover us. If only my childhood chums could see me now rubbing shoulders with the stars on a weekly basis! Alas, it ain't everything I dreamed it would be.

Hollywood, "the star of LA," is a small town and its social circles are even smaller. Once you start circulating in these industry cliques, you are, for the most part, "in there." No one stands in line, or pays for parties, in this inner sanctum. Queuing up to shell out $20 bucks for the club is a sure sign of greenness. That's why guest lists were invented. Now the nightclubs have started issuing out platinum cards to select people on their mailing lists. Membership does have its privileges! With these passkeys, the cardholder is granted VIP status: free admittance before a certain hour and access to the club's VIP room. Talk about egotrippin'! The way some of these cardholders act you would think they were waving around the keys to the city instead of a self-serving plastic promotional tool.

As soon as I learned the secret to gaining access to these soirees, I started attending them in heavy rotation. The trick is to get your name on one mailing list, or befriend a promoter, and the invitations start showing up on your welcome mat like needy children. Even though these mixers are glorified meat markets, they can still be good venues to network with big ballers. Highrollers are more readily approachable at the bar or dance floor of an industry party because they assume that you either know someone important or are doing something of note to be invited to these exclusive functions. And of course, there's always the possibility that a celebrity (your favorite male soap star, perhaps) will make an appearance and ask you to dance.

Thanks to my S.G., I was exposed to the clandestine world of LA industry parties. I've shared the ladies room with models, sat at the bar talking to directors and even got the opportunity to be felt up on the dance floor by a few struggling actors. I had come a long way, baby!

Sometimes, however, you have to be a little more innovative to crash certain posh parties. In other words, you have to get your scam on! At Magic Johnson's annual Mardi Gras, a girlfriend and I were posturing outside the gate, trying to gain admittance to this exclusive event. Tickets were $125 a pop! Everybody who was anybody was on hand for the gala and we were trying desperately to be in the house...pro bono. Even though the proceeds went to charity, we didn't have the funds to foot the door.

My friend and I pleaded with a promoter we knew who had tickets for the affair. As he made his way past us through the turnstile, he smugly remarked over his shoulder, "This ain't the club." His arrogance infuriated us and we were determined to show him that we had enough pull to get in the place.

We approached two slightly tipsy gray-haired gentlemen who were staggering out to the parking lot. My girlfriend explained our plight: we weren't hustlers, nay, but two enterprising writers who were trying to crash the festivities so that we could do an article on the event. The kindly grandfathers then pulled out extra tickets and escorted us through the turnstile. Actually, my girlfriend made it in, but as luck would have it, the man who was supposed to accompany me through the gates didn't want to give up his ticket. I stood on one side of the entranceway and my girlfriend stood on the other side, glaring at me impatiently. She's the kind of friend who would leave me there by my lonesome and tell me about the party afterwards.

One of the younger guards, a cutie pie, sensed my dilemma and gave me a gentle nudge through the portal. I caught up with my friend and we sashayed down the red carpet as if we were on the A-list of invitees.

Once inside, we passed the promoter who had thrown us shade. He called us "big ballers" and tried to rap to us as we sauntered past him and his friends. We were not checking for that party peddler. Laughingly, we called back to him, "This ain't the club."

Five Reasons To Attend Industry Parties

1. To make connections.
2. To get your star gaze on.
3. To test your LA Chic savvy.
4. To find Mr. Right (yeah, right!)
5. Drama, drama, drama!

Another industry soiree where I had to put my scheming skills to work was at a birthday bash for a certain unnamed soap opera honey. From across the room, I spied the Nubian prince and his procession arriving at the back door of the club. As they made their regal way up to the VIP room on the second story landing, I discreetly tried to join them. A burly, cock-blocking security guard obstructed my entry past the velvet rope. The ogre demanded that I produce a VIP bracelet or get to stepping. In a last ditch attempt, I summoned up the audacity to call the soap star over before he reached the top stair. I acted like I had known him all my life. Flossing my "sexy with attitude" voice, I beseeched him to help a sister out. Leaning his fine frame over the banister, he regretfully informed me that the club owners were hassling him because of the fire code and the inordinate amount of bodies already in VIP. In short, he could do *nada* for my situation.

Frustrated, I stood at the foot of the stairs, surrounded by a throng of screaming, adoring fans and trying not to be lumped in with the groupies. I looked good, my outfit was banging and I had connections. Didn't I have enough juice to get into the luminaries lounge? I had almost achieved celebrity status (in my mind) and I still felt like a commoner. It was a case of the Prodigal Daughter trying to get back to her royal roots.

As fate would have it, two mack daddies were standing on the step in front of me. I overheard them explaining to the guard that they were late-comers to the entourage. With a dazzling smile, I tapped one on the shoulder, saying that I would be their escort for the evening. Luckily for me, they didn't object. I linked arms with the dapper duo and we pushed through the crowd. The fiendish security guard eyed me suspiciously. He proceeded to pester me again about my lack of VIP credentials, but my saviors explained that I was with their party.

When I arrived upstairs at the much-celebrated VIP room, I got the shock of my life. There sat the soap opera stud...with an Italian cutie on his lap. I recognized her as a so-so actress on a mindless babefest television drama. Mama Mia wasn't letting my honey dip out of her sight, even going so far as to pull him away from a few fans who were asking for autographs. I was crushed. Here I had sacrificed my sanity and self-esteem to party with the man of my dreams only to be let down like this. It was a sad day for the fearless fly girl, indeed, but also a moment of eye-opening clarity.

Subconsciously, I had envisioned myself in the role of this charming ingenue who gets swept off her feet by a famous, dashing movie star. The fact that the leading man might already have a leading lady had not been written into my script.

When you get caught up in the world of glamour that industry parties provide for many sisters, it's easy to lose contact with your ho-hum, banal existence. Circulating in VIP circles, being invited to exclusive bashes and being within breathing distance of a celebrity can elevate a girl to star status (if only in her own mind). Entertainers, who other folks can only watch on television, or catch at a concert, are often within a hand's reach at these functions. I was almost on my way to becoming a stalker! Seeing the soap opera stud with his girlfriend was like having a bucket of icy water dashed on my daydreams. Luckily for me (and for him), I was able to retrieve my grasp on reality after that night and edit him out of my future fantasies.

I have actually left more than one industry party on the verge of tears. Even as I am getting dressed for the evening, pulling on my pants and putting the finishing touches to my makeup, I know that shortly I will be surrounded by the same phony females and bragging brothers. What am I searching for? Part of me just wants to get out of the apartment, away from my lonely world, and be a star for one night. I want to see and be seen. In my mind, I am not just a nobody from Norristown, PA, but a fabulous, jetsetting LA socialite.

Another part of me just wants to dance and let my body get carried away with the rhythm. The high school wallflower has blossomed into a twentysomething disco diva who wants to let the room have it! I'm making up for all those missed adolescent opportunities and storing away these musical moments for remembrance. It doesn't matter that I don't recognize half the songs the DJ is spinning, or that my dance partner is three inches shorter than I am and five years my junior. I am flaunting around my size seven frame with abandon, getting my retroactive boogie on.

Another smaller part of me is still *slightly* star struck and wants to see a famous face gracing the place. I'm looking fantastic, feeling fearless and perhaps I'll get lucky. Maybe some young, hot director has heard about my script and wants to get it produced. Maybe he's single and wants to get it on with me. Maybe all of my heart's desires will be fulfilled this evening, and maybe none of them will.

Retrieving my jacket from the coat check, I step out into the cool night air. I curse myself for wasting gas and a face full of makeup on what has, once again, proven to be a typical night of LA partying. As I hop in my truck, music blasting to drown out my sorrows (Tupac, take me home), I realize that industry affairs are a necessary evil. Teary eyed, I speed up the 101 Freeway towards the Valley, carrying this sad knowledge…I'll be back again next week.

Once I was able to put industry parties into their proper perspective, going to these mixers became less and less of an emotional onus for me. Particularly after I started writing about them for a living. The trick, especially for my out-of-town, disposable camera carrying friends, is to learn how to work a room and not act like so much of a fan. I've learned that the people who get the most attention at these functions are not the ones who flit from circle to circle trying to make their presence felt. The ones who can command a crowd are usually standing off in a corner of the room by themselves, observing the scene with a bored, important look, as if they are gracing this party with their presence for a moment before moving on to the next fabulous shindig.

If you do happen to approach a celebrity at these industry events, don't do it like a gushing groupie. Most stars are there to chill, anyway, but they appreciate honesty more so than adulation. The hardest thing for this small-town girl to swallow was that stars are real people. They go to the cleaners, to the supermarket, to the video store and (amazingly) to church. When I approached singer Chanté Moore at her album release party, I could have gone buck wild like many other fans around her, who were rapidly depleting the diminutive diva's oxygen levels. I saw the displeasure on her face, and knew she was about to let somebody have it. Smiling, I stepped to Chanté and told her that I used to attend her sister's church in San Diego. Grinning, she said, "That's also my church," and we had a brief conversation about how much we missed the pastor. I know that I probably made more of an impression on her than if I had just verbally oozed on about loving her latest album.

A word of caution: these industry parties are not for the faint of heart!

A good girlfriend was in town visiting me, and I made the mistake of inviting her to one of these mixers without alerting her to its attendant dangers. She, too, grew up in a small town and was excited about the prospect of hobnobbing with young black Hollywood socialites.

On the evening of her foray into the lifestyles of the rich and shameless, I advised my friend on what to wear (by then, I was an old pro at dressing LA Chic). We both wore ensembles worthy of a Hollywood vamp, our hair was hooked up and we had on more M.A.C. makeup than a ghetto cover girl. It was time to let LA have it!

My friend and I strolled into the party as if we had just come from signing a three-picture deal and made ourselves comfortable on a couch in the middle of the room. Now all we had to do was wait for the men to flock to us. Well, having lived in LA for two years, I knew the unlikelihood of this occurrence. However, my homey, newly arrived to the city, was unprepared for the ego-crushing event to follow.

We sat on that couch, making small talk and laughing at the hoochie mamas and trick daddies. There was enough synthetic hair and polyester clothing in that joint to alert the fire marshal. We sat pretty for hours and still no one approached us. We sat until the M.A.C. makeup began its slow slide down our faces and my friend's false eyelashes became unhinged. Still no one stepped to us.

My Baltimore-bred buddy made up her mind to circulate so that the room could get a better view of her and become enchanted with her dazzling personality and quick wit. Girlfriend struck out. She stepped to one of the many ball players in the house to ask him what the deal was. A brief and fruitless conversation with him convinced her that black women are not only *not* a hot commodity in LA, we are usually not even on the market.

Having become adjusted to the way some black men treat black females in LA (and besides, I was there on business), I brushed the lack of attention off. But my visitor was livid! She knew too well that if we had strolled into a club back on the East Coast, we would have acquired more phone numbers than an NBA draft pick and about as much clout.

After two hours of listening to my friend stew at the blatant disrespect from the menfolks, I thought it was high time to school her on...

CHAPTER 7
THE LA HIERARCHY

Color Scale: high yaller, yaller, high brown, vase-
line brown, seal brown, low brown, dark black.
—Zora Neale Hurston
"Story in Harlem Slang"

IT GOES without saying in LA that looks are everything. Some black men take that adage and elevate it to a way of life. Especially when it comes to dating.

Now I'm not trying to be a hater; if you've got it, flaunt it. But some brothers in LA choose to flaunt everything but a black woman on their arm. And if it is a sister they're sporting, you can best believe she's melanin challenged. I'd be willing to wager that not since the early part of the last century has the color scale been in such full effect. Back then, light-skinned blacks tried to prove their bluebloodedness with the paper bag test. If they were as light as or lighter than the bag, they considered themselves elite and shunned their darker-skinned brethren. At any rate, "The blacker the berry the sweeter the juice" is definitely a maxim seldom heard on the streets of LA.

At one popular hotspot on La Cienega, it is rumored that you have to be of a certain complexion to gain admittance. Armani-clad gatekeepers stand at the roped off entrance jabbing a thumb at certain females who have "the look" and granting them access to the club. One night, a dark-skinned diva stood cussing the bouncer out because a plethora of white,

Asian and Latina women had bypassed her on a line where she'd been standing for almost thirty minutes. I, too, have waited in line observing the chosen few who are blessed enough to make it past the velvet rope. For those unaware, the hierarchy goes something like this: white women, Asian women, Latinas, mixed-race women, light, bright, damn-near-white women and light-brown-skinned women. The few dark-skinned sisters who are able to foot the door are usually accompanied by a Superficial Girlfriend of the light-skinned breed.

Speaking of mixing races, jungle fever has reached bubonic plague proportions in LA. If you fall in love with someone outside of your race, that's one thing. But I have sat in functions where I was the only sister in the setting amidst couplings of black men and white women. Whatever happened to black love?

> *"In LA, being international is code for dating every color in the rainbow. Interestingly enough, I've found that most brothers who consider themselves 'international' out here don't include the color black in their kaleidoscopic courtships."*

At a barbecue that I attended one summer, a filmmaking brother (with dreadlocks, no less) was engaged in a conversation with me while his beautiful blonde wife sat lovingly at his arm. She smugly commented that they had read an article in the *LA Times* on how interracial dating in LA had reached an all-time high. Did Barbie think I was going to pass out a gold star to them for helping this city reach its race-mixing quota? I ain't mad at her for snagging a handsome brother, but the audacity of some white women in this town is palpable. They can be downright bold. I have had several white women try to push up on black men who I am out with while I am standing right there. It's as if they know that they are validated daily by black and white men, and they wallow in this feeling of self-importance like a security blanket.

At a listening party that I attended for a certain chronic-smoking gangsta rapper, several Melrose mommies in the room were fawning over the thugs, while giving my sisterfriend and me the evil eye. My girlfriend remarked bitterly, "Why do they always have to be at our functions?" I'm no proponent of reverse discrimination, so I shrugged her comment off. White women infiltrating black events is so commonplace in LA and most are more hip to black culture than sisters nowadays. But the babes at the gangsta rapper's party should have had "O.G." branded on their foreheads for "Original Golddiggers." They knew too well that if they had encountered these same black, cornrowed hustlers in a dark alley, or on an elevator, they would have been clutching their Prada purses and secretly dialing 911 on their cell phones.

When I am driving and encounter black couples walking hand-in-hand, I almost ride off the side of the road in shock because the sight is such a rarity in this city. It is not uncommon to go into Roscoe's, that beloved urban eatery, and encounter tables full of black women eating by themselves. The brothers are usually lounging in the corner with Heidi. Or Ming Lee. Or Guadalupe.

I was once told by a black male friend, whose baby's mama is white, that I am not "international." In LA, being international is code for dating every color in the rainbow. Interestingly enough, I've found that most brothers who consider themselves "international" out here don't include the color black in their kaleidoscopic courtships.

There is a lot of self-hatred going on in this city. A sisterfriend of mine was visiting her two white girlfriends and their black roommate, a modern day "Three's Company." The black roommate told her that she was the only black woman he had met who was on his "level." He also managed to fix his mouth to say that he didn't date sisters because they were too materialistic and only washed their hair once a month. My girlfriend had to leave the apartment posthaste before she inflicted bodily damage on the moron.

This young woman, whom I consider my little sister, doesn't have many black female friends or role models. She doesn't think it's strange that all of her white homies have black boyfriends, are fluent in Ebonics, and clock black culture as regularly as rappers sampling beats. I'm flattered that certain white women are taking an interest in lifestyles outside of their own, but cultural borrowing (and sometimes, downright hijacking) is so common in this city that it's almost alarming.

Is there a secret pact between black men and white women in LA that sisters aren't up on? I was at a club talking to a black male friend who made the comment that while he doesn't date white women, he could see why so many brothers are flocking to "the other side." He pointed out that the white women on the dance floor had just as much rhythm as the sisters and much better figures. Laughingly, he told me that the white chicks had bigger booties than me (which is no great accomplishment, let me tell you). I had to listen to his tirade about black women not taking care of their bodies. Alas, at the gym, all he saw next to him on the Stairmaster was Becky getting her Olivia Newton-John groove on, while Shaquita was somewhere down the street raising her cholesterol level at Fatburger. Never mind that his own pot belly was protruding over his belt buckle. It's frightening that black women are held to such a tighter standard in LA than in other parts of the country, oftentimes at the expense of their own physical and emotional wellbeing.

I'm an open-minded woman, but sometimes I think my sense of nationalism may be a little outmoded. Especially in La La Land. When you speak of wanting to be in a relationship with a black man, folks tell you you should be more "international," "universal" or "humanist." I'm fine with people getting it on with whatever race they choose. It just saddens me to see so many Nubian queens being passed over on a daily basis, myself included, for the flavor of the month, which is most likely vanilla. Or vanilla swirl.

Having an understanding of this pecking order helps to combat bitterness. In no way do I condone this preferential treatment. It just helps me cherish myself more as a beautiful black woman and makes me realize that certain brothers struggle with the male equivalent of the Dysfunctional Diva syndrome. The air out here isn't just toxic to sisters. Surprisingly enough, black women in LA get more play from white men and foreigners who see us as "exotic." Go figure.

To all my sisters in the struggle, country-born or city bred, there is still hope for us in LA. There is that rare breed of man who loves and respects the black woman in all her hues and complexities. I haven't found him yet, but I know he's out there somewhere, just waiting to include me in his mix. And that brings us to the subject of...

CHAPTER 8
CALIFORNIA COURTSHIP

---

*"I can always be distracted by love, but eventually
I get horny for my creativity."*

—Gilda Radner

DATING IN LA is a curious sport. We go into it hoping for the best, preparing for the worst and settling for anything in between.

When I first moved out here, I was dateless for almost a year because I knew that most men in LA wouldn't touch a woman over a size six. It wasn't until I lost weight and started going out on the regular that I realized how lonely I was. Up until that point, "Girl's Night Out" was the only ritual keeping me going.

If you've read this far, then you realize how crazy the dating game is for black women in LA. When I first moved to this city, I just knew I was going to be widely successful and find a husband, who was also going to be widely successful. Can somebody say naïve? Had I lived in Atlanta or New York, I'd be happily married with my 2.5 kids by now. But since I reside on the Left Coast, I'm geographically challenged.

While I don't subscribe to that sobbing school of "Lawd, when I'se gonna find a good black man?" a sister still can't survive on nights of one-handed romance and *Good Times* reruns. I was sick of the comments "When you gonna find a man?" and "When you gonna get married?" People were dropping subtle hints about my sexual orientation and my advancing age. I knew I had reached the point of desperation when an older white woman on my previous job tried to do some matchmaking. This woman has a good heart, but most white chicks don't have a clue about their black girlfriends' taste in men. They think that as long as the man is black and has a pulse, he's acceptable dating material. As soon as my former coworker said my potential blind date favored Ben Vereen, I knew I was in trouble. Needless to say, I respectfully bowed out of the date.

Telltale Signs You're Dating An LA Man

1. When the bill comes at a restaurant, *he's* the one who runs to the restroom.
2. His shoes, hat and blazer are color-coordinated.
3. He's vertically challenged.
4. He doesn't know your number by heart, but his agent is on his speed dial.
5. You can't get the home number, but you can get the digits to the cell phone, the beeper and the two-way pager.

The unavailability of male companionship in this city can drive even the most level-headed woman to some crazy lengths. I know my mother raised me right, but since I've been in LA I've dated a college student seven years my junior (to this day, I'm still not quite sure of his sexual preference), a car-salesman-turned-realtor-turned-drug-dealer, and a few other losers. Now some sisters may say "Yeah, but it's like that all over." I concur for the most part, but in LA, brothers seem to be on a whole nother wavelength. I've met men originally from the East Coast who moved to LA and assimilated. They would complain about how hard it is to find a good black woman in this city—one who wasn't a gold-digging mommie, or a wig-wearing weirdo—then they'd turn around and become the male equivalent of the Dysfunctional Diva.

Take one brother I know who moved out here from Chicago to make it in the film industry. He was purporting himself to be the epitome of a good black man: goal-oriented, a good provider and a sensitive listener. A woman would be foolish to overlook the great qualities he possessed, qualities which he delighted in showing every woman he met. Every woman except his wife, that is. She hadn't yet made the move to LA from the Windy City.

While I was still in San Diego, right before I made the journey to LA, I had been corresponding with a brother in North Hollywood who owned his own magazine. We had never met in person. Even though I spoke with him frequently on the phone about freelancing for his publication, I briefly entertained the possibility of something more than just a working relationship.

When I finally moved to North Hollywood and he saw me in person for the first time, I'm sure he got the shock of his life. I was not the sexy-voiced hottie he had envisioned, but a frumpy cow with a bad weave. His interest in me, professionally and romantically, plummeted in direct proportion to my ample waist line. After that initial meeting, he never called me again. I insisted to my friends that the reason he cut off all contact with me was because of my weight, but they maintained that he had simply found someone else for the job. After all, he was a good Christian brother with his own magazine and radio talk show. Shame on me for thinking he could be so superficial.

As luck would have it, two years later I ran into that same good brother at an entertainment convention in Palm Springs. He hadn't seen me in awhile, so he strolled right past me. When I called his name, his face went through a complete metamorphosis. He kept gushing about how much weight I had lost and how I looked like a completely different person. I'm sure I could have thrown some panties at him then, married man or not, but I just smiled politely and kept on stepping. I realized that my dimensions had changed, but his hadn't. He was still the one-dimensional person from two years ago.

The sisterfriends that I've talked to about the lack of suitable men in LA have complained of the same problems. These brothers will start off decent enough, then flip the script.

Some men might complain that it's easy to be led astray in La La Land because a lot of sisters don't have respect for themselves. I agree with that theory to a certain extent, especially while viewing the way some women belittle themselves to get the attention of a man. Walk into most any night club in LA and you'll think you're on the set of the latest gangsta rapper's video; the only thing missing is the Olympic-sized swimming pool. At some clubs when certain songs come on, don't be surprised if you're flashed by some anonymous woman's G-string. At one party, I witnessed one bold sister taking a man's penis out of his pants and jerking him off to the beat. That kind of behavior could cause a brother to act buck wild, but if he's a self-respecting man in the first place, he won't allow himself to be led into temptation.

Another reason some brothers tell me they won't settle down in LA is because women outnumber them by like 10,000 to 1. With ridiculous statistics like that, what red-blooded male would be crazy enough to let himself get roped into a relationship? Even ugly men, who ordinarily would have to bribe women to talk to them, come to this city and get downright cocky. To make matters worse, LA is home to some beautiful women; this city is Model Central.

One 22-year-old black male, who I view as my little brother, confessed that he doesn't date black women because he's intimidated by them. For him, Latinas are more easily approachable and don't demand as much from his limited paycheck. Sisters in LA, he's told me on more than one occasion, are too high maintenance for his budget. If they're not high classed hotties, then they're hoodrats.

I feel sorry for young black women in LA having to grow up under these stereotypes. Believe me, it doesn't change as you age. I know very few sisters in this city who are happily married or in healthy relationships. Most women I know aren't looking to trap some man into marriage. They're just looking for some genuine companionship, someone to rub their feet after a long day, or to cuddle with at the movies. Dating in LA is such a strange conundrum. You have to worry about competing with all the beautiful women in this city (black, white and other) to find an available brother who isn't still living under his mother's roof. Then when you find one, you have to worry whether your looks and figure are good enough to keep him. At the back of your mind is that ever-present fear that he may be trying to date one of your girlfriends (or worse, one of your guy friends). With all those issues to worry about, it's enough to drive a good man away when you finally find him!

"Men are from Mars and women are from somewhere south of Long Beach," jokes comedian/actor D.L. Hughley when I talk to him about the crazy dating game.

"I don't think that men talk about relationships as much as women. When we talk about relationships, it's how come Kobe and Shaq ain't getting along. A man can ride in a car with another man and say two words in a day. If you ride in a car for fifteen minutes with a woman and you haven't said anything, y'all having a fight."

I'm not trying to discourage those who live in LA, or are relocating here, and have high hopes of finding Mr. Right. Just know what you're up against, ladies. Hey, as long as Greyhound still runs, and the airlines stay in business, you can always import a good man from out of town. As for me, I'll probably end up being in a bi-coastal relationship...

CHAPTER 9
BI ANY MEANS NECESSARY

"Bisexuality is not so much a copout as a fearful compromise."

—Jill Johnston

SPEAKING OF RELATIONSHIPS, LA has its share of non-traditional couples. I've been propositioned by more sisters in this city than I have men. It's flattering to be considered attractive by another woman, but still a disheartening reality to know that other sisters find me more desirable than the brothers do.

Something in the air out here just makes women want to get free or experimental. More than a few sisterfriends have admitted to me that they've had bisexual encounters, or at least seriously considered sleeping with another woman. It's not an uncommon sight to see sisters strolling down the street arm-in-arm, or gyrating together on the dance floor.

Telling people I live in North Hollywood sometimes raises eyebrows because this neighborhood is known for having a large gay population. Folks in LA will assume that you're "twisted" until proven innocent. I've had my sexuality questioned more than a few times.

I went out once with a good friend, a college buddy of hers who danced in a club, and several of that girl's fellow strippers. As the ten of us crowded into the limo on our way to the restaurant, one thin, blond-wigged chick in the group announced to me, "I like big women like you."

If she thought that I was going to be flattered by that remark, she had another think coming.

> *"I love all sisters. In fact, I consider myself one of the most vocal sistergirl advocates I know. Even though I joke about our peccadilloes, I think all black women are beautiful."*

At the restaurant that we went to, the now defunct Shark's Bar, all eyes were on us. We were dressed like we had just come from a Li'l Kim video shoot. Brothers were flocking to our table, trying to find out how they could be down. I was with some really gorgeous women that night, albeit hoochies, and their beauty seemed to rub off on me.

We went to a nightclub after dinner and had a ball dancing with each other. The spirit of freedom was contagious and other women on the dance floor were trying to get jiggy with us. Now in LA, some women dance together just to get attention from the menfolks, but we were really enjoying each other's company, *sans* the brothers. If I was living back on the East Coast, I don't think I would have had the courage, or the desire, to be dancing cheek-to-cheek with another woman. Strangely enough, since I've lived in LA, that evening was the closest I've ever come to female bonding. Go figure.

One night I went to Peanuts, the widely-heralded female strip club, which is known for attracting gay women. A gay male friend had invited me to the club for a female rapper's birthday party. At first I was on guard as usual, fearing that people would think I was twisted, or worse, that the female denizens of the strip joint would try to step to me. Secretly, I wanted to get a glimpse of the female rapper. Rumors of her escapades with other women had been circulating for years and my nosy self wanted to see if there was any truth to them. She wasn't the only one I had heard racy rumors about. Several other popular female celebrities, some married with children, have been known to make the rounds at Peanuts, and I was on a mission to see if I could "out" any of them. After being in the room for thirty minutes, however, my inhibitions and petty curiosities flew out of the window. We were all just getting our groove on, enjoying the universal language of music and each other's fabulous company. I didn't get to meet the rapper that night, and even if I had, I would no longer have been interested in her sexuality. I guess I'm just a humanist deep down inside. After that night, I decided that her sexual preferences were her own business.

Not all same-sex encounters can be pleasant ones and you have to know how to handle yourself, preferably without getting cut or maimed.

I was kickin' it at a party in Compton one night with my model friend. To be such a dainty diva, she frequents some rough hangouts. After the club, we stopped at a pool hall a few doors down so that she could use the restroom.

The moment we footed the bar, I was on edge and ready to go. Maybe I was just feeding into the stereotypes about that area because had I been at a pool hall in Beverly Hills (if they even exist), I wouldn't have thought twice for my safety.

As I sat primly on a couch in the corner waiting for my friend, I felt the only other woman in the room staring me down. She was rocking a skintight leopard-skinned body suit with colored contacts to match. As she swaggered across the floor towards me, I knew that I wouldn't make it out of the bar alive. Here I was, Miss Hollywood, acting all prissy and proper, hadn't even opened my mouth to speak, and I was in *her* neck of the woods. The sister surprised me by sitting next to me on the couch and saying, "You sho are pretty." Then she kissed me long and lingering on my cheek, much to the laughter and catcalls of the dozen men in the room.

I knew that embarrassing me was her way of infighting. My next actions would determine whether I would leave the bar intact, or wearing her cue stick up my butt. I was either going to have to kiss her back, or cuss her out for fronting me. Both options scared me witless.

Fortunately, my clubhopping cohort chose that moment to appear from the bathroom. Because she is beautiful, people mistakenly assume that she is fragile as well. But this vixen is more Crenshaw than Melrose and she welcomes a showdown more than a fashion show. She assessed the situation, then bopped over to us. Grabbing my hand in one of hers, and the woman's hand in the other, she began dancing with both of us to the music streaming from the jukebox. She told my would-be attacker that her eyes were beautiful, and that the woman looked just like Lauryn Hill. Well, the sister ate those comments up and offered to buy us both a drink. Luckily, my friend and I were able to escape from the bar unscathed.

I love all sisters. In fact, I consider myself one of the most vocal sister-girl advocates I know. Even though I joke about our peccadilloes, I think all black women are beautiful. If a sister has on a banging outfit, I'll tell her she looks good. Since I am booty-challenged, if a black woman walks by with a nice shape, I'll compliment her on it, and tell her I wish I had a butt like hers. Some black women may hold back on praising others for fear of being labeled "twisted." It's easier to talk about how busted a sister's weave is than how pretty her smile is. But we need to start validating and affirming each other more. If we don't, who will?

I'm including this chapter to let you know that in this city, you can find sisterhood in the strangest places. She may be your next-door-neighbor, coworker, or even the president of your...

CHAPTER 10
FAN CLUB

"A monkey never thinks her baby's ugly."
—Haitian Proverb

I GREW UP in a female-headed household. Our tiny rowhome was usually filled with the laughter of my mother's friends and women family members. These ladies were ultra-confident, strong and doing it at the highest level. Most importantly, they had my mother's back. Whether she needed someone to cook dinner for my brother and me while she was at work, yell at us (or whup us) when we misbehaved, or just sit down and reminisce about old times, she could call on her girls.

One thing that struck me like a sledge hammer when I moved to LA was the fact that the closest family member was 3,000 miles away. This meant no home-cooked meals, no one to fuss at me when I got out of line and no one to have my back. One of the ways I've dealt with not having any family close by is by having a fan club, my own cheering section. For those sisters new to town who have no relatives in LA to rely on, I highly recommend taking the time out to establish a support system.

I have witnessed firsthand how having a fan club can give one Mad Confidence and bolster a girl's credibility. An entourage, you ask? Nay, a group of friends who believe enough in your skills that they can network for you in your absence and create a buzz about your talents (real or imaginary).

> *"One great secret of survival in LA is surrounding yourself with a few people who understand your passion and want to help you make it happen. In essence, you have to form your own surrogate family."*

A financial advisor from my old job used to make his living as an actor. He had a twenty-year entertainment career and a lot of invaluable industry contacts. An actress friend was looking for an agent, so I decided to pick the brain of this actor-turned-broker.

When I approached the ex-thespian about my friend, he asked me to describe her work. I began hyping up the wannabe leading lady so much that I felt like I was her publicist. I neglected to tell the man that I had never seen my girlfriend act. One thing I can't stress enough is that LA is the home of hyperbole. The more exaggerated your story (told with Mad Confidence, I must add), the more people will buy it.

Another girlfriend of mine, who is a choreographer, had been putting a bug in my ear about a singer friend for whom she did backup dancing. The chanteuse, recently signed to a major label, was in town performing at a club on Sunset, and my friend invited me to catch her act. I had been treated to press releases and head shots of the singer, so I figured it would be to my advantage to see the girl in action.

The nightclub was packed, and I knew a good buzz had been generated by my friend for her singing friend. Since she was also doing publicity for The Diva, my dancing friend had rustled up a good amount of bodies to fill the club. Then The Diva sashayed onto the stage. I cheered with the rest of the crowd because the dance moves were on point and the costumes were fabulous. And then The Diva opened her mouth.

Now I know I'm tone deaf, but nobody's signing me to a record deal. So what's the difference between The Diva and me? She was lip synching to her CD (which kept skipping) and her shrill vocals were enough to straighten the hair on the nape of my neck. I looked around in amazement to see if anyone else thought they were witnessing the Second Coming of Paula Abdul, but the audience was feeling her. They were screaming like mad and nodding their heads to the music. I had to question if something was wrong with my musical tastes. Maybe I was too old to appreciate good "sanging." Then I realized that most of the people cheering were Fans. They had been brought in by my dancer friend to lend credibility to The Diva's performance.

Another great secret of survival in LA is surrounding yourself with a few people who understand your passion and want to help you make it happen. In essence, you have to form your own surrogate family. Now these folks may be as crazy as can be, but what family doesn't have its share of loonies? These people are usually in the same industry that you aspire to be in, and believe that your success guarantees their success. Hence The Diva's eminent fame ensured that my choreographer friend would be doing some fancy footwork in at least three or four of her music videos.

Once that concept clicked for me, I began cheering The Diva until I was hoarse. I knew she lacked talent, but she had Mad Confidence to make up for her scarcity of vocal skill. Knowing how hard it is for the black female to not only crack open Hollywood's door, but get over in the entertainment industry, I secretly applauded The Diva. She had finagled her lack of talent into a lucrative record contract written up by some white execs sitting in corner offices lined with plush leather furniture. And besides, there might be some press releases or feature articles that I could write about her. I could add "Publicist" to my resume. Yes, in LA there is...

CHAPTER 11
NO BUSINESS LIKE YO' BUSINESS

LA has the rest of the world beat on shameless self-promotion and inflated job titles. To this day, my Rolodex still contains business cards from the CEO of a management company (who dayjobs as a driver for FedEx), an accomplished actress (who temps as a file clerk) and a filmmaker (who incidentally asked to borrow $10 from me at the time of this writing).

No one has a real job in La La Land. I was reminded of this phenomenon when I went back East for a visit and was strolling around the mall with my mother. It was two o'clock in the afternoon on a Wednesday, and I noted with incredulity that there were only ten other shoppers in the place besides us. On any given weekday afternoon at the Beverly Center, or any other mall in LA, the store looks like a marathon. Unwittingly, I turned to my mom and asked, "Where is everyone?" She looked askance at me and replied, "At work."

Most people I know in LA are just sitting around waiting for the Big One to hit, making as great an impact on their financial Richter scales as the quake of '94. You can't toss a rock without hitting someone aspiring to be in the business. My apartment building alone is like the black Melrose Place. I've rode the elevator with actors, shared laundry detergent with producers and sorted my mail side by side with backup singers.

I felt like a fool because I was working full-time at an investment firm and all of my friends were unemployed. When I would come dragging in the door at five o'clock, world-weary and emotionally whipped, my unemployed neighbors would shake their heads at me, eyes dripping with sympathy. How, they would wonder, did I let myself get corralled into working 9-to-5 for The Man? Didn't I take a bus trip across country (with an 18-month layover in San Diego) to gain my fame as a writer in LA? I wasn't being true to my art. The day should be utilized pounding the pavement with my portfolio until my writing was able to pay the bills. And speaking of bills, could I lend them $60 so DWP wouldn't cut their lights off?

However misguided these words of wisdom were, I was able to siphon out this tidbit of advice: you have to have your own side business to survive out here, otherwise the pain of your day job will crush you. Struggling isn't always about not having enough money; sometimes it's about working at a job that diminishes and patronizes your true talent.

> ### *Business Essentials*
>
> 1. Laminated business cards bearing headshots
> 2. Beverly Hills PO Box
> 3. Leopard skinned business card holder
> 4. Website with more headshots
> 5. Inflated job title

I was slaving at the investment firm for two lazy white men whom I was smarter than. Whenever I tried to elevate my secretarial status by proposing ideas to help make the company run more efficiently, these two *Wall Street Journal*-reading, prematurely-balding slobs would shoot me a stare that said, "You don't get paid to think. Just keep the coffee coming." When I told them I was taking screenwriting classes at UCLA in the hopes of selling a script, I could just hear them thinking, "You'll be here for awhile." I would shuffle in my door every night, throw myself across the bed and cry in frustration. My talent was stagnating and I didn't know how to go about jumpstarting my writing career.

Finally, I couldn't stand the madness any longer. I had come to Cali with two suitcases and a dream, and no meager office job was going to hold me back from achieving it. One night, with cardstock purchased from Office Depot, I sat at my computer and printed out my very own business cards. The cards were simple; no flashy graphics, curlicues or headshots. They just touted me as a "Writer" and gave my contact information. And they worked wonders. No more would I stand around at industry parties devising ingenious ways to elevate the ignoble administrative work I performed at the investment firm. I was a Writer. Period.

The beauty of having a business and business cards is that people take what you say at face value. You are a director even though you could never afford the DGA dues, and the closest you came to directing was when you showed your mom how to hold the camcorder at your cousin Yolanda's wedding. You are an actress, even though your one "movie" is an infomercial that only gets airtime at three in the a.m.

One young sister, who recently graduated from a college on the East Coast, relayed to me her disenchantment with the lack of black-owned companies on the Left Coast. I reminded her that most sisters I met out here had their own businesses; whether or not they had a *physical* office space was another issue. Sisters in LA don't let particulars like zoning laws and business licenses dissuade them from doing their thing. A public relations guru I know has turned her apartment into an office. And my image consultant friend is a walking advertisement for her business. She just goes wherever the fashion-challenged call her.

In the biggest display of Mad Confidence that I've ever exhibited (with the exception of my bi-coastal journey to La La Land), I decided the time had come for me to quit my job at the stock brokerage to focus on my writing career full-time. As I proudly handed in my resignation notice, my bosses were flabbergasted. Had I finally sold a script? Where was I going? "Away from here!" was my smug retort. They didn't need to know that I didn't have another job waiting for me and no money in the bank. This girl was determined to show the world that she could make it after all. The homefolks on the East Coast thought I was nuts for giving up a stable job and steady income, but my LA friends thought I was finally maturing.

As luck would have it, I was only unemployed for a short while. Two weeks after I walked away from my old job, I strolled into a new position, this time as Editor of a radio trade publication. I couldn't believe my good fortune. Someone was actually going to pay me to circulate with the celebrities! My new boss discovered that writing was my first love and he even encouraged me to make contacts for myself if it would help to further my screenwriting career. He didn't have to tell me twice. At every industry event that came around, I was up in the house, bolstering my Rolodex of entertainment contacts. Now I had a legitimate reason to be mingling with the stars.

I have to admit, I felt a little sad trading in my trespass for a press pass, but after two years of anonymity, I finally felt as if I was making a name for myself in LA. Even though I was safely back in the working world, I still couldn't stifle my...

CHAPTER 12
HUSTLING SPIRIT

"All women hustle. Women watch faces, voices, gestures, moods…She's the person who has to survive through cunning."

—Marge Piercy

AS I'VE SAID earlier, sisters in LA have to hustle because no one else is going to do it for them. Even women I know who have agents still have to do their own legwork if they want to achieve a modicum of success. Hustling can be summed up with this ghettoism: "A closed mouth don't get fed."

It tickles me to think of how shy I was when I first moved to LA. It didn't take me long to learn, however, that people equate timidity with stupidity in this town. Then, too, I realized that the task hardest for us to face is usually the thing we have to conquer in order to achieve our dreams. My challenge was shyness. I was geek in my high school and known as the wallflower at parties. Even in college, the thought of taking a mandatory public speaking class as a freshman seriously had me considering sitting out for a semester. But I knew that I would have to overcome my timidity and fear of talking to other people in order to network in this town.

One hustling tactic I've discovered for getting over in LA is that you have to walk into a room like you own it and act like you have every right to be there. This was a lesson I had to learn over and over again as door after door was closed on me.

I was invited to a listening party for chanteuse extraordinaire Patti LaBelle and wanted to make her acquaintance. The Philly crooner was in another part of the room that was exclusively roped off for the ultra VIPs, but I was determined to speak to her. A girlfriend and I strolled up to the velvet rope and smiled winningly at the guard standing sentinel behind it. He wasn't having it and sent us on our way. We watched in disbelief as a male friend of ours flounced up to the doorman and was immediately granted access to the VIP room. Our honorary girlfriend turned around, beckoned to us and told the guard that we were with him. The man let us pass without a murmur. I reasoned that the guard must have known my honorary girlfriend, but he later told us he had never seen the guard before in his life. "Honey," he drawled, "I just strolled up to him like I knew where I was going and he knew not to mess with me!"

A few months later, I had the occasion to test this theory out to see if it truly worked. One rainy Sunday afternoon, I was trying desperately to get on the set of "Soul Train" (Don't laugh; I'll explain why in a minute). I wasn't on the list, I wasn't a dancer and I didn't know anyone at the door. I had never been on the set before, and I pulled up to the guard shack to ask directions. Peering in my window, the burly security guard asked if I was a dancer. I hesitatingly told him I was, despite the fact that I had on more clothes than an Eskimo. Then he smugly replied that it was a little late for me to get on the show. I finally broke down and told him I was a freelance writer and I just had to interview Shemar Moore, who hosts the show. This melted the guard's resolve a little. He said, "Well, since you're kind of cute, I'll see what I can do." He led me through a little maze until we reached the section where Shemar's people were sitting. I stood against the wall as the man tried to process my presence through the proper channels. After a short wait, the guard beckoned to me and said, "Come this way." Elated, I thought he was going to take me to Shemar's dressing room, but instead, he led me back out to the sidewalk in the pouring rain!

Mentally, I slapped myself for trying to go about things "the right way." Crushed, I stood on the sidewalk by my car, trying to figure out my next move. Suddenly, my honorary girlfriend's words came to mind, and I snuck around to the other side of the building. I stopped two dancers on their way out and explained my plight. They told me to go to the side door, ask for "Bill" and he would take care of me. Summoning up enough attitude to rival that of any prima donna, I sashayed through the rain past two other security guards and into the side door. As luck would have it, I ran smack into the same fool from the guard shack (he must have been on the lookout for me). Staring him straight in the eye, I said, "I'm here to see Bill, and I'm not leaving this building until I find him." A page standing nearby heard the defiance in my voice and went to find Bill for me as I took a seat. The page returned a few minutes later and, to the chagrin of the cock-blocking security guard, escorted me into the studio.

Hustling can have a dual meaning: it can mean doing everything in your power to get what you want, or it can mean trying to constantly get over on other people. Most of the folks I've met out here fall into the latter category.

Since most LA dwellers are struggling to be famous or rich in some capacity, it stands to reason that they will do anything to ensure their success. And that means knifing their friends in the back in the process. I've let several "friendships" whither away once I sensed that I was being hustled. Once I lost weight, brothers weren't the only ones who wanted to be in my company again. Female "friends" who had never invited me anywhere and didn't know what it was to return a call, started blowing up my phone. Since I had given myself an image makeover (and had a good job getting invited to exclusive entertainment events), it was now acceptable to be seen with me. It was extremely hard for me to sever ties with certain people since I didn't have any family and less than a handful of confidants in the city. But once I realized my own self-preservation and self-worth was at stake, I had to tell those back stabbers to get to stepping.

Since I had put the word out that I was a screenwriter, I was getting offers from other industry hopefuls who wanted to team up on writing projects with me. One would-be writing partner thought that we could collaborate on a screenplay. I later discovered that homegirl had no writing experience, but thought the great equalizer was her entertainment contacts. Her idea of a partnership was for me to do all the writing and for her to do all the conceptualizing and socializing. At first, I was content to struggle through the screenplay with her. Later, as I beefed up my own Rolodex, I decided it wasn't worth the effort.

One good friend of mine, a stylist to the stars, can tell a few horror stories about being hustled. My honorary girlfriend is fabulous! His hair looks better than most sisters I know and his skin is flawless. Because he has such a high wattage personality and is known to beat a face and hook up hair, celebrities naturally gravitate towards him. This diva is in demand in Hollywood, but his sweet demeanor makes him an easy target for hustlers.

My buddy had befriended one high-level television executive and styled her hair often. He considered her a good girlfriend and would often be "on call" for this high post sister. Eventually, she started taking advantage of my friend, getting him to do her hair at all hours for bargain basement prices. One thing led to another and he ended up cussing the executress out and ending their relationship.

Folks were aghast that he stood up to this network queen. Wide-eyed, they would ask my honorary sisterfriend if he feared the woman's wrath since she has mad connections, and there was always the threat of her blackballing him in the industry. In reply, my friend would roll his eyes (like the true diva he is), suck his teeth and state that he knew as many people as she did and had a much better rapport with them. The only thing the executress had over him was a few more zeroes in her bank account.

Another well-known singing siren whom he styled and traveled all over the country with tried to pull the same stunt, making him work on demand, and thinking his time was her time. He eventually cut her off as well, but learned what goes around comes around. Since the termination of their relationship, this buxom belle has since gone through three other stylists. She has since gotten back in touch with my friend, begging him to travel with her again and style her wigs. He respectfully declined. He has learned to not always make himself available to these hustlers. Now he calls the shots.

"I hate being labeled a bitch," he admits, "but if you act too nice in this industry, people will walk all over you." One of his favorite sayings is "Sometimes being a bitch is all a person has to hold on to." It works for him.

Hustling shouldn't always be a negative experience. There are positive ways to scheme. Since I was having about as much luck finding an agent as OJ was in finding Nicole's "real killers," I had to connive to get my screenplay out there. I managed to get myself named as "Creative Consultant" on a director friend's film and went around telling people that I had movie experience. They didn't need to know that I had no clue what a "Creative Consultant" did as long as it got my screenplay across their desks.

Even when I had a legitimate job in the industry as Editor of the entertainment publication, and had a reason to be dealing with celebs on a daily basis, I still had to use my hustling skills on a few occasions. One such time was when I wanted to interview a certain actor for the magazine. I had seen him out at a few industry parties and knew that he was approachable. I wanted to go the legit route, however, so I contacted the firm that represented him.

Because the magazine I work for is a trade, and is geared toward specific markets, the woman I corresponded with at his management company had never heard of it. I was determined to get the interview, so I sent her a media kit with a few issues of the publication.

I called a few days later to make sure she had received the package. From her smug tone, I knew she was throwing me shade and probably thought that my magazine wasn't big enough or worthy of an interview with her client. I heard the dismissal in her voice and quickly flipped the script. In other words, I hustled her. I told this cock-blocking babe that I had seen her client out at a few functions and that he had expressed interest in doing the story. Yeah, right!

"I know I've met you before," I lied. "I was invited to a party in his honor and I saw you there."

"I was there!" she gushed. (Score one for me!) "I think I've met you before, too!"

As it turns out, I was just taking a wild hunch that she'd be at his party, but since she represents the star, why wouldn't she be in the house? Then as luck would have it, she and I were both friends of the promoters who threw the bash, and they were best friends with the thespian cutie. Like they say in LA, connections are key. By the time I got off the phone with the chick, she was treating me like we had known each other all our lives. Needless to say, I got the interview.

Most folks in this city believe in credentialing. Sometimes you have to give the people what they want…even if it isn't the whole truth. A divafriend who works at the *LA Times* has found that just the mention of her company has opened doors for her; she doesn't even have to give her title. We were at a mixer that was jam packed and I urgently had to use the restroom. Unfortunately, security was not allowing folks re-admittance to the VIP lounge. Well, this sister has a weak bladder, and I was more than willing to forfeit my quasi-celebrity status for a trip to the ladies room. Grabbing my arm, my girlfriend informed the guard that some ladies from the *LA Times* were in the house and needed to use the restroom. The brother at the door made a quick attitude adjustment. We were escorted out of the lounge and when we returned from the restroom, we were ushered back in past the throng of folks at the door.

Even though it's nice to throw around titles and company names to get in the door, my experience has proven that it's sometimes best to just approach folks on an even keel. People appreciate honesty and can smell the schmoozers a mile away. When I finally interviewed Shemar Moore in person (Heaven help me), I wasn't gassing his head up and falling over him (although I did remember to pack my inhaler in my purse). I asked him what had been on my mind for awhile, and what other people were probably thinking: Did he get to where he is in Hollywood simply because he's beautiful?

"Soap opera has a certain stigma behind it. It's the land of beautiful people; it's the land of silicone and receipts," he laughs. "Pretty might help me get in the room, and that's great. I'm flattered that people want to call me pretty, and call me a sex symbol and call me a hunk. But I know that pretty and hunk status is not what's kept me in this game for seven years. Hunk status did not get me an Emmy," he points out. "I've been in the game for seven years, and I'm going to be here a while longer. Sooner or later, y'all are going to notice that I'm bringing something else besides how I look."

I think the reason I have always been attracted to those who have made it, and the telling of their stories, is because they represent where I strive to be, and their struggles make me aspire to greatness. It's nice to be able to interact with celebrities from time to time (even though they're just real folks like us). Photo ops are cool, if that's your thing, but on the real, my main goal in life is to be...

CHAPTER 13
A LADY WHO LUNCHES

PEOPLE IN LA don't eat. Or rather, they go out to restaurants to social-
ize, but the choice of cuisine is the least of their worries. It's the ambiance
that determines the restaurant. When sisters in LA go out to dine, they
think of location first, how likely they are to see and be seen (and be
picked up by a baller), and how the food tastes.

I grew up in a family that loved to cook. Unfortunately, I never learned
that valuable skill; I was too busy sampling the dishes. Unlike their Left
Coast brethren, people on the East Coast live and love to eat. Dining out
is such a pleasurable experience back home because of all the delectable
dishes to be had. I grew up only twenty minutes from the greatest Philly
cheese steaks and hoagies in the world (called subs in LA). When I lived in
Baltimore, I seriously reconsidered my bi-coastal move for fear of leaving
behind the fabulous Maryland crabs.

Having said that, I want to warn you that there are no great eateries
in this city. Sure, Mr. Chow in Beverly Hills has some bomb Chinese
cuisine (if you can afford the price tags), Miyagi's on Sunset is the place
to go before the club for sushi, and for the soul food crowd, there's
always M&M's restaurant or Reign. But LA isn't known for its fine
food. When my out-of-town guests are visiting, they are usually treated
to such five-star restaurants as McDonalds, Popeyes, and that old stand
by—Burger King!

Foods LA Turned Me On To

1. *Carne asadas*
2. *Smoothies—can't live without my Citrus Squeeze!*
3. *Veggie burgers*
4. *Kimchi—the Korean equivalent of collard greens!*
5. *Persian rice*
6. *Lumpia (A Filipina sisterfriend hipped me to this delicacy!)*
7. *Falafel*
8. *Greens with tofu*
9. *Soy ice cream*
10. *Chicken and waffles (in my pre-vegetarian days!)*

Moving to the Left Coast has been a definite culture shock to my palate. The city is a veritable melting pot in terms of cuisine.

I've eaten Ethiopian, Thai, Indian, Mexican, Korean, Greek, Persian, Vietnamese; you name it. Whenever I'm fortunate enough to be invited over a girlfriend's house for dinner (most sisters out here only know how to make reservations), I find that they are much more carefree with their cooking than their East Coast counterparts. At one homey's house that I dined over, I was treated to collard greens with tofu, pasta primavera and a burrito. Talk about cross cultural cuisine!

I have a Korean sisterfriend who can burn better than some black women I know and will fix you a plate even if you are just stopping by for five minutes. This Asian honey first turned me on to kimchi—pickled cabbage. At first I regarded the spicy Korean delicacy as if it were a fungus, but now kimchi ranks up there with collard greens. You know that's saying something! If you are striving to be a lady who lunches and a diva who dines in this town, you need a healthy dose of flexibility.

I do have to give LA props for being one of the few cities I've lived in that has restaurants willing to indulge my vegetarian appetite. At a soul food diner that I visited in Ladera Heights, the waitress didn't blink an eye when my breakfast order consisted of homefries prepared with no butter and a vegetarian taco on the side with no cheese. At Real Foods Daily on La Cienega, vegans rule! Any would-be diner who asks for butter or cheese on their food might be shown the front door posthaste.

Top Five LA Restaurants

1. **Roscoe's House of Chicken and Waffles.** Would you like some greens with your maple syrup?
2. **Real Foods Daily.** For the vegetarian in you. The seitan fajitas are the bomb!
3. **Mr. Chow.** Tasty Chinese Cuisine, and the place to be to star gaze.
4. **Reign.** Soul food goes Beverly Hills.
5. **The Stinking Rose.** You want some food with that garlic?

I visited New Orleans, that fabled city of Creole cuisine, for a radio convention. It was my first journey to Louisiana, and I was shocked to discover that all menus seemed to consist of some flesh food soaked in butter. When I asked the waiters to serve me something without meat, they looked at me as if I had just put roots on them. I couldn't wait to get back to LA where my vegetarian tastes would be indulged without a complaint.

Truth be told, I didn't just come out to LA and become a health nut, even though this city does encourage such transformations. When I first moved here, I was hipped to some real Cali cuisine, like salsa poured over cream cheese (used as a dip for tortilla chips) and chicken stewed in chocolate. When I really assimilated to LA living, I started making my daily rounds on the fast food circuit like most of my girlfriends. It was only when the cashiers started recognizing me at the drive-thru windows of Popeyes and McDonalds and I couldn't stand to look at myself in the mirror anymore that I made a conscious effort to incorporate healthy eating habits into my life.

That aside, I want to make it clear that eating in LA can be a pleasurable experience if you don't focus on the food. Many deals are made over lunch and dinner. People treat you with more respect if you know the finer restaurants in town and can quote from their menus by heart. It's also a good way to get together with your homies and bug out over the craziness in this city.

I remember sitting on the patio of Chin Chin's on Sunset with one girlfriend, just people watching and star gazing. She was pretending that she was the host of her own Fashion Faux Pas show. Using her knife as a microphone, she was the one-woman fashion police, giving out tickets to all style offenders who passed our table. I was reliving the fearless reporting lifestyle that I had known back in Baltimore and was interviewing my friend as if she was a major star. Well, in her eyes, she already is.

Dining together can serve to bond us. Another experience that may help you better relate to your sisterfriends in LA is having...

CHAPTER 14
A PLACE TO WORSHIP
(BESIDES YOUR MIRROR)

"Strength and honor are her clothing; and she shall rejoice in time to come."
—Proverbs 31:25

SOME SISTERS in LA are surprisingly spiritual. Even if they go clubbing on Saturday night, they still manage to sashay into the sanctuary bright and early Sunday morning to get their praise on.

Churches in Los Angeles are daunting to say the least. Being raised in a conservative 200-member Methodist church in Phoenixville, PA, I was amazed to learn the place of worship I had chosen out here boasted membership 10,000 strong and advertised four or more services on Sunday. Definitely something for everyone. There were also huge television monitors mounted at all four corners of the sanctuary for those who wanted a chance to see the pastor getting busy in Technicolor. As if that wasn't enough, hanging in the vestibule was a prominent sign, "Please turn off your pagers and cell phones before you enter the sanctuary." Only in LA!

Nothing compares to the preaching I have heard in this city. At one church that I visited on La Brea, the pastor dropped more slang than a gangsta rapper and postured about as much. He was really getting jiggy with it! Glimpsing around to see the reaction of my fellow congregants, I noticed necks nodding in agreement with the minister's words. The Spirit so moved one sister that she was out in the aisle, cabbage patching for the Lord. Then I noted the lack of gray-haired mothers and fathers of the church and the proliferation of Via Spiga, two-way paging Generation X-ers and Y-ers in the pews. The pastor was really in touch with his parishioners and he was tailoring his message to fit their lifestyles.

> *"Happiness is rooted in the word 'happening,' which means we don't experience 'happiness' unless something is 'happening' that we want to happen. And when the 'happening' stops, we stop being happy. But joy comes from acceptance, gratitude, faith and appreciation...Joy comes from seeing the good and seeing God in every situation."*
> **—Jewel Diamond Taylor**

Initially, I felt removed from this stadium-like setting and such unorthodox preaching. Had I been at church in an ordinary town, say Norristown, Pennsylvania, such a spectacle would seem unfitting, if not downright sacrilegious. But I came to the realization that this is how people "do church" in LA. It was to be expected. Not surprisingly, some of the divas I had met at the industry parties attended the same church as I. Hey, a girl's gotta worship somewhere. Clutching monogrammed Bibles to their chests, and waving their sculptured nails heavenward, they praised the Lord unabashedly, tears tracking a muddy course through their M.A.C. makeup. It was easier to identify with the women at these times, and I saw them as more human. We were all at the altar for the same reasons: lost angels wandering in search of a home, in search of family. Even if we weren't obeying all the tenets of the Bible, we were still keeping it real by doing our part on the Sabbath.

What I came to understand is that these glitzy vixens were just empty vessels, as I was, and they just wanted to come to a place to lay their burdens down. A sanctum where they wouldn't be judged or criticized. Life in La La Land is draining for a sister, to say the least. Strolling around every day, hustling to maintain, perpetrating as if you are someone else, trying to succeed in a town that almost guarantees your failure—all these factors can wear on a sister's spirit. Maybe that's why we are always the ones who shout the loudest up in the sanctuary.

I'll never forget one experience that changed the way I viewed church in LA forever.

When I first moved to town, and before the ink had dried on my lease, I began experiencing major health problems. I didn't have insurance, so I went to a clinic where I was diagnosed with adult onset asthma. The fact that I was overweight didn't help my condition. When I would lay down in bed at night, it felt as if a heavy hand was pressing on my throat, strangling me. I would wake up every two hours gasping for breath and eventually had to cough up $75 bucks for an inhaler to combat these chronic attacks. Even though I never traveled without my trusty inhaler in my purse, the wheezing episodes would leave me totally incapacitated. They could wake me up out of a sound sleep and have me fumbling for my medicine before my eyes were completely open. I thought these attacks were God's way of telling me I had messed up bigtime by moving to such an ungodly city.

It got to a point where the inhaler ceased being effective. I had to start using a nebulizer, a machine the size of a shoe box that administered my asthma medicine in mist form through a long tube. I couldn't go more than two hours without sucking on this hated device. I discreetly carried it around in a gift bag whenever I went to the movies, dinner or library, and refused to go anywhere that didn't provide me with direct access to an electrical outlet. My illness became a constant source of embarrassment for me.

Before that first month in LA was up, the paramedics had made three early-morning visits to my apartment. I was given oxygen, an EKG and advice on how to treat my condition. They never took me to the hospital because without medical insurance, I knew I'd have to give up my first-born child to pay for an emergency room visit.

I was saddened by the strain my illness was having on my mother 3,000 miles away. Any unanswered telephone call she made to my apartment and Moms was on my voicemail, frantically threatening to call my land-lord or the police to make sure I was still in the land of the living.

I have to give props and a plug to my neighbor friend, who is the direc-tor of the film *A Lover For My Husband.* He has saved my life on more than one occasion. He was the only person I had befriended in the city, and I can remember knocking on his door at three in the a.m., nebulizer in tow, knowing that he had to be up early for a temp assignment. My friend knew the routine. He would open the door groggily, then go back to sleep on his futon while I plugged up my machine (which made almost as much noise as a vacuum cleaner). I would tremble on the floor by his feet, hoping I wouldn't perish before morning came.

I'm sure the fear of dying alone far outweighed the fear of dying itself. I had no family and exactly one friend in LA. How typical of me to travel all the way to La La Land just to die on the wrong side of the world.

I also think I was mad at God for allowing me suffer so. I was 27-years-old, and when I should have been enjoying the prime of my life, I was forty pounds overweight, I had a debilitating illness and had to lug around an annoying apparatus because I couldn't breathe on my own.

I was certain the Angel of Death was knocking on my door and, sooner or later, I'd have to let him enter. After a particularly frightening asthma attack, I woke up one Sunday morning determined to get to church. At least if I died in the sanctuary, I'd have the pastor present to perform last rites. And I wouldn't be alone, I'd have 10,000 mourners by my side.

The preacher's message that morning dealt with endurance. He stressed how hard it is to survive in LA and said that some people die emotionally and spiritually every day. He kept repeating the phrase, "You're not going to die. You're not going to die" over and over again that I knew he had to be speaking to my own situation. At that point, tears rained silently down my face like Noah's flood. I have always been self-conscious about crying in church, but that day I completely lost my composure. The sister next to me, sensing my internal turmoil, hugged me fiercely, and began praying fervently for me. No other place in LA but in church would a woman embrace another woman, a stranger no less, and speak words of peace and encouragement to her spirit.

From that point on, I began incorporating regular church visits into my routine. The preacher was right; I didn't die. The Lord knew I had to get my book on survival techniques out to sisters everywhere and He put my asthma in check. After three months of being on a vegetarian diet, I shed the forty pounds that had plagued me for so many months. Although I still carry my inhaler in my purse, I haven't had to use it, or my nebulizer, since September of 1999. Now my mother and I both rest a lot easier at night. As she is so fond of saying, "Child of God, you've come from a mighty long way." Amen!

Whatever your religious preference, be it Jesus, Buddha, Allah or whomever, it's still good to find a place out here where you can worship and feel that you're part of a community, and not just existing in the city with no roots. As long as you live in Lost Angels, your faith is going to be tested on the regular. Drugs, hustlers, free sex and shady friends are prevalent in La La Land, and it's a good idea to fellowship with sisters who endure the same stressful situations. Most of the women I've befriended in LA aren't from here and regular spiritual interaction serves to bond us tighter than weave glue.

Speaking of bonding, another experience that I count on to help keep me grounded is holding onto my…

CHAPTER 15
GHETTO PASS

"Among poor people, there's not any question about women being strong..."

—Dolores Huerta

SO MANY SISTERS who have relocated to LA complain about the "lack of culture" in this town. Yet, they fear traveling far from Melrose and Beverly Hills to seek it out.

To keep it real, and keep myself down to earth, I still visit the 'hood. Yes, the hood, which boasts some of the best culture a girl could hope for in a city such as this.

The California African American Museum on Figueroa in East Los Angeles is a great place to visit and also a repository of black culture. I went there for the first time to cover an event honoring the multitalented Gordon Parks. Parks is the director of movies such as *The Learning Tree* and the original *Shaft*. The feisty octogenarian filmmaker also enjoyed an illustrious career as a brilliant photojournalist, and his exhibition "Half-Past Autumn" was on display at the gallery.

While strolling through the museum, you can see the original mirror from singer Ella Fitzgerald's dressing room, and beautiful paintings from prominent African-American artists. It's a great reminder that we can aspire to be more than perennial clubhoppers and ghetto socialites.

Leimert Park in the Crenshaw District is another excellent place for divas to get back to their roots. On a nightly basis, you can stroll through the black-owned business community and hear poets blow in coffee-houses, listen to John Coltrane wafting through the open door of a restaurant, or watch the old timers (and new jacks) show their prowess in chess. Contrary to what one sees in 'hood movies or hears on the nightly news, these are some peace-loving folks. In fact, the last place I would expect to encounter violence is in Leimert Park because its inhabitants know about self-respect.

One of the reasons I love the East Coast is because the black women that I befriended there are so enlightened. They owned their own homes and businesses, were conversant on politics and love and seemed impervious. Flighty women like me need strong, self-empowered women in our corners to validate and uplift us.

When I moved to the Left Coast and encountered a legion of flaky females like me, it stood to reason that I would have to either a) be the strong one in the relationship (imagine that), or b) seek out some women who resembled the role models that I missed back home. I found these role models in Leimert Park. These sisters wore their own hair: dreaded, braided, or twisted up in some fierce Afrocentric 'do. They were playwrights, directors, poets, actresses and writers. They either lived in or frequented this part of town to hone and display their craft.

People in the inner cities know something about pain. Since LA is just a big 'hood, it stands to reason that the respective experiences of these artists would be woven into a tight cloak to both comfort and shock their audience.

In Leimert, I've sat in a room full of black folks and watched film shorts produced by black women. They were bringing the African-American diaspora to a whole nother level. I've heard fearless sisters who were poets wailing their blues at the Underground Railroad, the World Stage or Wrapture, and was even inspired to write poetry of my own. I've stood inside the historic Babe & Rickey's Inn at two in the a.m. and listened to a sepia chanteuse blowing like the second coming of Billie Holiday. Her music was a welcome change from the frenetic Hip Hop and house beats piercing my eardrums on a weekly basis at the clubs and industry parties.

It was in Leimert Park that I was challenged to take my screenwriting to the next plateau. Up until that point, I was shopping my scripts around, futilely trying to find an agent. But there is a forum of screenwriters and directors that meets monthly in that area and I got the chance to network with other writers who had produced their scripts themselves. At one of these gatherings, I sat next to famed actor/director Bill Duke and relayed to him my struggles to sell a screenplay. Bill encouraged me to shoot the script on my own and once completed, he assured me that he would attend the premiere.

Now his advice sounds like an oversimplification of the directing process, but I've known writers/directors who have filmed their shorts for under $1,000 and have won awards at film festivals. I'm taking Bill's advice, and am in the process of writing my first short, which I hope to direct some day.

All of this may sound as easy as cake, but it's been an uphill battle for me. I haven't given up hope, because the secret I've learned is that agents, directors and the like have been trained to...

CHAPTER 16
JUST SAY NO

"I wrote for twelve years and collected 250 rejection slips before getting any fiction published, so I guess outside reinforcement isn't all that important to me."

—Lisa Alther

WHEN YOU REALIZE that most screenplays are probably used to wipe up coffee in this town, and many actresses have more restaurants listed on their resumes than roles, then you can put your own chances of success into perspective.

After completing two screenwriting courses at UCLA Extension, I finished my first real script and hit the pavement with it. I was so hopeful back then! My screenwriting instructor once told me that one couldn't throw a brick in this town without hitting an agent, and I set out to discover if her words had any truth to them.

Having gone to school with the brother of a famous rapper/actor, I was delighted to discover that my old college chum was working in town not far from the Beverly Center. I visited him with the hopes of garnering some interest in my screenplay. We chatted over cocktails at a restaurant across the street from his building and the conversation seemed to be headed in the right direction. We returned to his empty office to rap some more and wound up in his conference room listening to CD's. My friend turned up the volume on his stereo and started dancing seductively in front of me. The music pumping from the speakers mounted in the corners of the room drowned out any further talk. At that point, I knew the conversation was definitely moving away from business.

I tried to segue back to my screenwriting aspirations, but my friend cut me off. In so many words, he told me that it was difficult, nay, impossible to make it in this town and he couldn't give me any referrals. I was devastated. Here gyrated the man who used to send Christmas cards to my father. I wasn't begging him to hook me up; I knew that he probably turned a deaf ear to many pleas from "friends" who wanted to get close to him because of his celebrated sibling. But we went to Hampton University together. I wasn't some gold-digging hoochie (maybe my chances to succeed would have been greater had I jumped up on the conference room table and started doing the butterfly); I was a talented writer trying to make it in the celluloid jungle.

Living in the shadow of his big brother's success, my friend had never had to struggle. Yet, there he danced, smirking in my face with this bored executive look and telling me how difficult it was to open the doors to Hollywood. Whatever! I realized then that the game was going to be a lot harder than I expected.

A very successful broker at the investment firm where I once worked played golf with a lot of celebrities and was very well connected in the entertainment industry. When I told him that I was a writer (by then I had two scripts under my belt), he took pity on my plight and referred me to a client/friend who was an agent. I was overjoyed! My first agent referral.

I called the agent and she instructed me to messenger my script over. Two months went by and I still hadn't heard from the woman. I sent her my second script with a short note, hoping that she wasn't buried under an avalanche of screenplays. A few weeks later, she called back saying that she absolutely loved my screenplay and her agency was thinking of sending it to Disney. I jumped for joy! I was almost in the big leagues, getting my turn at bat. She wanted me to come in and interview with her and her partner in person. I knew I had hit pay dirt, because most agents don't want to see your face unless they are about to make you a serious offer. On the drive to her office in Santa Monica, I was already spending the money I would make from the sale of my first script.

My initial disappointment came from the size of her place. It is said that you can pretty much tell how big of an agency you're dealing with by the way the office looks. She was working out of a small, one-room boutique about the size of my living room. But I thought that if she could work hard and get a script sold for me, I didn't care if she operated out of her bathtub.

I sat with her and her partner for over an hour, parlaying questions from both of them: How long had I been writing? What background did I have? Yadda, yadda, yadda. Then they kept asking me if I liked to write characters other than the ones I wrote in my first two scripts. Translation: Did I only write about strong black characters overcoming challenges or would I be flexible enough to write a screenplay that featured mentally-challenged Negroes? I had written an intelligent script that dealt honestly with the lives of black folks. It wasn't a hood or hoochie movie and maybe that's why I went wrong in their eyes. They loved my writing style, but in order to get known in Hollywood, they wanted me to write something a little more white-folks friendly. Needless to say, I scored a big fat zero that day, and crossed that agency out of my Rolodex.

It's so hard to keep your integrity as a writer when you know so many agents are always looking for the next 'hood comedy. In a conversation with comedienne/actress Mo'Nique, who has her own sitcom "The Parkers," I asked for some survival tips sisters need to stay in the game. A fellow transplant from Baltimore, and a full-figured goddess as well, Mo'Nique knows about how shady the industry can be, particularly to black women who don't fit into this city's stringent standards of beauty.

"African-Americans in Hollywood still have a long way to go," she says. "There is a lot of unfair treatment, but instead of us complaining about it, we have to do something about it. The very first time I came to Hollywood, I got an agent who said to me, 'Let's be honest with each other. You will never be the star. You will always be the girl next door, the funny cousin, but never the star.' And I said, 'You will never be the agent for me.'"

Mo'Nique is an enigma in this town because she is a voluptuous black diva calling the shots. She knows something about survival.

"Never have a Plan B; stick to your Plan A," she stresses. "A Plan B makes it easier for you to give up. You have to say, 'I'm going to make it or I'm going to die trying.' People used to ask me, 'What are you going to do *if* you become famous?' I would always say, 'I'm already famous, you just don't know it yet.' That's the attitude you have to have."

Fellow comedian Bill Bellamy corroborates Mo'Nique's advice, saying, "Every African-American female who's trying to come up in the LA game has a horror story, but you have to really believe in yourself. Forget how many No's you get, because I still get No's all the time. You still have to believe in yourself."

Dealing with discouragement goes hand-in-hand with trying to make it in the industry. There's some shadiness on both sides of the fence. We expect the producers, directors and higher ups not to be in our corner, but it hurts that much more when someone on our level makes it, then refuses to reach back and pull others up. Several neophyte television writers who recently cracked open Hollywood's doors have acted very evasive when I've asked them how they managed to get in the game. It's as if they feel threatened that another black presence is going to diminish their position on the team.

A girlfriend from Philly recently asked why it was taking so long for me to sell a script. If she only knew! Girlfriend thinks you just mail your screenplay to an agent and wait at the mailbox for them to send a check back to you. She doesn't know that you have to hustle with all your spirit (without giving up your soul) just to get your script on somebody's desk. Then you have to pray that the powers-that-be don't use it as a door stopper, or to sop up their spilled espressos.

When I was taking screenwriting classes at UCLA Extension in 1999, the room was filled with other industry wannabes hoping to make a mark on Hollywood with their scripts. There was only one other sister taking the course with me. The pages that our class workshopped from her script were pretty good, but I was confident that I would be the first to sell a screenplay. Imagine my surprise when, not too long ago, I turned on the radio and heard that her script was being made into a movie and Lauryn Hill was slated to play the lead. I was shattered! Her script was little more than an upscale 'hood movie. I just knew I could write circles around homegirl, so how come Hollywood wasn't biting?

What's really hard in this business is knowing that you have talent and watching other less gifted individuals pass you by. Many meaningful projects get passed on while the more mindless ones get the greenlight. One such brother, who earns a ridiculous salary as a television sitcom writer, confided to me that he knew his plots were overly ghettofied. But hey, a brother has to get paid.

Speaking of major money, the opulence of these young, urban socialites just leads me to believe that LA is really…

CHAPTER 17
THE LAND OF THE
FLOSSED

"It is easy to be independent when you've got money. But to be independent when you haven't got a thing--that is the Lord's test."
—Mahalia Jackson

THE FLOSSING LIFESTYLE that is so prevalent among young black socialites in this town can be overwhelming. You know who I'm talking about: those Rolex-rocking, cell-phone toting, Motorola two-way paging, sports car driving folks who are the main decision makers in this city.

At an LA Laker party that I attended with a girlfriend, we sat next to some ballplayers and noticed the inordinate amount of attention they were giving to their two-way pagers. The sister across from us sat on the couch with a bored look, playing with her PalmPilot and iggin' the brother at her side who was trying to rap. We noticed one industrious brother on the dance floor getting his boogie on. Suddenly, he paused in the midst of his two-stepping to answer an incoming call on his cell phone. The music at this function could have rivaled the cacophony at a Metallica concert. This man had put his groove on pause, completely disrespecting his dance partner, to hold a conversation, which in all likelihood, he could not hear. Glancing around, it seemed as if everyone in the room had some communication device in hand. My girlfriend and I, who didn't even own cell phones, felt like rejects from the caveman era.

Is it just me, or does it seem as though these "communication" devices are just tools to floss? Very little communication seems to be getting accomplished nowadays. I remember back in high school the rage was pagers. Brothers who knew all of two phone numbers (and probably didn't even have a telephone at home) had pagers hanging flagrantly from their hips. Not to be outdone, sisters started getting into the game, too. Even though they were proud of their newfound toys, they would get downright attitudinous if someone they didn't want to talk to was blowing up their beepers.

Believe it or not, I received my first preparation for this flossing lifestyle in college. When I went to Hampton University (which is just a microcosm of LA), I was inundated by the wealth of my fellow underclassmen. Knowing I couldn't afford to participate on my mother's income, I was depressed on a daily basis. I seriously contemplated killing myself. Well, maiming myself, anyway.

Come move-in day at Hampton, the parking lots at the dorms would look like a presidential cavalcade, filled with Jaguars and Porsches. My self-esteem and self-worth would plummet in direct ratio to my new roommate's bank account. I would hear my classmates bragging in the corridors about the bomb estates and plush manors that they hailed from. This one's father was an architect and that one's mother was the CEO of a Fortune 500 company. I didn't even know what my mom did for a living!

My aunt Dottie was instrumental in helping me to see through these flossing facades. She would scoff at the jetsetting behavior of my peers and their families, remarking "The cars are probably leased and they're probably one day away from foreclosure on the houses." As for the job titles? "They're probably janitors calling themselves 'maintenance engineers,'" she would laugh.

Well, Aunt Dot's theories were pretty much on the money about Hampton and they hold true for a lot of the ballers in LA. But I'm hardheaded. Sometimes, I have to relearn information…over and over and over again.

There is a saying in the black community that goes "Every shut eye ain't sleep and every good-bye ain't gone." Translated: "Everything is not what it seems." I'd like to add my own modification to that maxim: "Every television appearance ain't fame and every high performance sports car ain't paid for." I know promoters riding around in V-12 sports cars, yet sharing an apartment with roommates. A pretty well-known comedienne/actress has a starring role in a television show that's on the air right now (at the time of this writing). She lives in my neighborhood. Now, I don't live in a bad community, but it ain't Bel Air.

It just goes to show that even though people have the trappings of fame and eminence, they might be struggling just like you and I. But being exposed to such opulence all the time (especially if you can't touch it or aspire to attain it), is enough to take a sister through a...

CHAPTER 18
PRE MID-LIFE CRISIS

"I have been in Sorrow's kitchen and licked out all the pots."

—Zora Neale Hurston

AN ETHIOPIAN girlfriend confided to me that she saw a lot of sisters in LA walking around defeated. In her country, black women were put on pedestals. In LA, however, she didn't notice the same level of respect given to her American counterparts.

Her comment made me realize how many sisters I see on the regular suffering from low self-esteem. A lot of it stems from, I feel, having to deal with this city's standard of beauty, which is unattainable for most black women. Now some sisters will dispute me up and down, refusing to admit that they are trying to be black Barbies. But I know black women in LA who have the numbers of cosmetic surgeons on their speed dials. One sister I met was trying to round up as many girlfriends as possible to visit her plastic surgeon in Tijuana so she could get a discount on her next cutting session.

I'm not just speaking about women strolling around cosmetically altered. I'm talking about women walking through life frustrated, disappointed, disillusioned, bamboozled, led astray, run amuck. I feel for my sisters because I have been where they are, and I am where they are.

When I interviewed Dominique DiPrima, daughter of fiery poet Amiri Baraka, and hip host of LA's top-rated "Street Science" program on KKBT

The Beat, I asked for her thoughts on the self-esteem issue among black women in LA.

"We are not upheld in the media as the ideal ultimate woman," she says. "Look at images of us in the mainstream media and even in our own Hip Hop videos. Young women need to see that there are different roles for us to have in life. We have to be the kryptonite. We have to be the antidote for all the poison that's constantly aimed at black women."

I agree with Dominique's theory that we need to reach back and uplift young black women. When I first relocated to California, a girlfriend and I founded It Is Written Literary Services, a program that teaches creative writing workshops to pregnant teenagers. The purpose of our project was to provide an outlet for their anger and frustration through the spoken and written word. Many of the girls didn't have any role models; they hated themselves and hated us even more. Several of them were semi-literate. A few had parents on crack, boyfriends in jail, and uncles, or other male family members, who had sexually molested them. The mentality of the girls in this program was enough to keep me teary eyed after every session. These young love-starved ladies didn't know the meaning of the word hope, so how could they teach it to their own babies? Their resentment of my partner and I was so strong that it was almost palpable. Perplexing enough is that the same mentality present in those twelve-and thirteen-year-olds is the same mindset that I find in a lot of black women my own age.

One girlfriend, who recently moved out here, commented that sisters in LA don't speak to one another. I was with her at the mall when she complimented a stranger on her shoes. The chick barely opened her mouth to say "thank you." Even though it might seem like a dangerous sport, my friend still goes out of her way to make eye contact with every black woman in her range of vision and engage them in small talk. It's a good practice that I also attempt to incorporate in my daily outings. At first, some sisters will regard you like a Census worker, but when they realize your intentions are genuine, they will open up to you.

A word to the wise: don't move to LA with sleeping pills or razors in your purse, because this city will most definitely tempt you to use them!

When I first relocated here, I think I was on the verge of emotionally dying. I had sacrificed my career as Editor of a newsmagazine in Baltimore to eke out a living in LA that was hazy at best. I didn't have any money saved. I was staying with friends, sleeping on their couches if I was lucky, or their floors if I wasn't so lucky. I still hadn't found my niche, and I was doing what a lot of LA dwellers do best: sowing creative wild oats.

I've spent a total of four years in The Golden State. Now, on the verge of thirty (at the time of this writing), I sometimes feel that I'm going through a pre-mid life crisis. Most of my friends back home are raising families. All I seem to be doing is raising eyebrows about my career aspirations. Even the old neighborhood bully from Norristown is now a successful salon owner, and the town trollop (who has several baby daddies) found someone nuts enough to marry her. Wasn't I supposed to be the first home-town girl to make good? Sometimes it feels like an uphill battle, but if I were to call it quits now and move back to the East Coast, I really would be starting over from scratch. The clock is ticking...

It doesn't help that LA is an ageist society. For those Generation X-ers over 30, some folks feel you need to be put out to pasture. And if you've reached that age with no real loot in the bank, or haven't made a name for yourself in the industry, Heaven forbid! You'll feel as if you're walking around with a big "L" plastered on your forehead for "Loser."

I was telling an acquaintance that a former co-worker, who is 39, hates her job as an Executive Assistant and is looking for another position. He smugly went on to say that she could hang her job search up because if one isn't firmly established in their careers by age 30, they are basically rejects, and no sensible employer will hire them.

In the face of opinions like that, I wonder what the future holds for some folks I know struggling to break into the industry: a 39-year-old receptionist/singer just now starting to shop her demo; a 33-year-old clerk/actress still going on auditions and a 37-year-old day laborer/filmmaker who has been trying for six years to complete his first feature film. Even those who are established in their careers by 30 are still not guaranteed stability in this fickle industry. Case in point, a 34-year-old writer friend got the boot from a teen television show because his writing was deemed "too earnest." Translation: the kiddies weren't feeling it.

On the East Coast, my friends with "normal" jobs are quick to wonder why their LA counterparts throw away their lives chasing dreams. By 30, the folks back there are home-owning, diversified portfolio having, 401 (k) planning people with little time to be wasting on impractical job pursuits. They could never contemplate the life of a 37-year-old filmmaker renting an apartment while whittling away his life savings to produce a movie, which may never get picked up.

Facing 30, at the time of this writing, is starting to become a major hurdle in my life. Do I lie about my age and start using anti-wrinkle cream? Do I rip up my VIP club cards, trade in Tupac for Deepak and start playing Bingo? A 23-year-old friend attempts to snap me out of my PTD— Post Twenties Depression. In one breath, he tells me I should be proud of my accomplishments by this age, while in the next breath, bragging that he hopes to be retired by my age.

What it really boils down to is a case of the grass being greener on the other side of the condo. My dear friend back in Baltimore, who is raising a daughter, would love to come out to Cali to try to make it as an actress. She's living vicariously through me. Meanwhile, here I am wishing I had someone to call me "Mommy." Are we ever really satisfied with our lives?

Every day living in this city can take a sister through emotional road rage. You strive so hard to stay on the freeway of life to wherever your journey may take you, and all the while other drivers are passing you by, cutting you off, or rear-ending you. Truth be told, I've felt like doing drivebys on more than a few folks.

Because the need to succeed out here is so great, a lot of sisters set irrational expectations for themselves. Forgive me for getting up on my soapbox, but I feel this is one of the most important issues in this book.

Message: There are so many talented and capable black women in LA who feel they are unworthy and incompetent because they can't jimmy Hollywood's door. They either act this out by mistrusting other sisters, or refusing to live up to their true potential.

I have a friend who, in my opinion, is highly successful. If Hollywood ever awarded "Most Likely To" titles, she would win Miss Congeniality hands down. Homegirl knows a lot of people in the industry, has a bomb personality, and is very talented as a reporter. This diva has the gift of gab and is not afraid to open her mouth to people. What's astonishing to me is that she doesn't see herself as victorious. She feels useless because she can't compete with the materialistic mommies that she sees so frequently on the streets of LA. My homey gets stuck in these dead end jobs that she hates and then complains about not utilizing her talent to its fullest potential. I want to give girlfriend a clue: Your gift is staring you smack in the face. You just have to stir it up!

Luckily for me, I've formed my own mini support group with other divas out here who are going through their own crises. One young poetic sister has helped me to see that imposing unrealistic time constraints on your success will just set you up for unnecessary stress. When 25 passes, then 30 approaches and you haven't inked a seven-figure movie deal, or made *Ebony* Magazine's "Fifty Most Influential" list, you feel like a flop. It's easy to develop a player-hating mentality and envy the success of your peers. I'm guilty, but the fearless fly girl is working through her issues. I had to let go of the mindset that once a sister makes it in Hollywood, she takes away from the already diminishing pie for other black women in this town. Like the chick from my screenwriting class who sold a script before I did. I eventually had to give her props on her accomplishment and keep on putting my own thing down. At the time of this writing, my screenplay is on the desk of an agent at William Morris, one of the top agencies in this town. They only accept projects by referral. Even if homeboy uses my script as a door stopper, the fact that my work was invited through the esteemed portals of the William Morris Agency is one of the major high-lights of my career.

LA is the Big Apple of the Left Coast. If you can make it here, you'll make it anywhere. Some may admire what I'm doing and some may say I'm California dreamin'(let's face it; you bought this book, so you at least thought I was a semi-expert on survival). Whatever you label me, you can't take away the fact that I'm living my life the way I want to so that I'll have no regrets when I'm 90. Right now, I'm still young enough and foolish enough to make this thing work! I'm still determined to survive in this city, although some inquiring minds might ask...

Epilogue

WHY BOTHER?

"If you're not living on the edge, you're taking up too much room."

—African Proverb

PEOPLE ask me all the time: If it's so hard to make it in LA, and good men are scarce, people are plastic, agents are shady, the food is horrible and road rage is running rampant—why do you insist on staying there?

Good question. I ask myself that time and time again. When a friend who I thought was a friend knifes me in the back, and another agency sends me a rejection letter, and I'm rolling solo (again) to the club and the brothers pretend I don't exist—I, too, wonder why I don't just pack my bags and hop that midnight train to Norristown.

LA is creative purgatory. There are so many souls wandering around in artistic limbo, praying that their talents will grant them all-access to the next station and hoping they won't get burned in the process. Until I get promoted to that next plateau, I'm going to stay on my creative quest.

Sometimes I feel like a mixture of Dorothy and E.T.—the need to go home for this small-town alien is staggering. I still lie awake some nights, or cry myself to sleep, but as long as I can phone home, I'll be alright.

One thing I'll always have to fall back on is the knowledge that I wasn't supposed to make it in LA. A fat, small-town girl with no contacts, no friends, no family, and most importantly, no LA Chic wardrobe, wasn't supposed to survive in this town for one minute. I consider myself a diva cheerleader: If I can be a success story, there's hope for everybody!

Forgive me for saying so, but something about LA feels so *right* to me. Maybe because I'm a flighty person to begin with, the incongruities of this town resonate in my being. You can take the girl out of LA, but...you know the rest.

When I'm driving down Sunset on a sun-splashed fall afternoon and see the beautiful Hollywood Hills looming in the distance...above an ad for liposuction—that is LA. When the only pleasingly plump woman at my gym is walking on the treadmill...and talking on her cell phone—that is LA. When I'm driving down the 101 Freeway, pointing out the Hollywood sign to my out-of-town visitor...and a high speed car chase, complete with a police phalanx, whizzes by in the next lane—that is LA. When my hairdresser confides that he has just written a screenplay and is also taking acting lessons on the side—that is LA...and I love it!

Not everyone who moves to or visits this city will become as enamored of it as I have grown. But one thing I can promise you, you definitely need survival skills to get through just one day in La La Land. The right mental and emotional armor helps to make this city more diva-friendly. Before you know it, you'll be a fearless fly girl in no time!

You've Been In LA Too Long If...

1. You rock sandals in December.
2. Traffic on the 405 doesn't bother you.
3. Your friends back home say you sound like a Valley Girl.
4. You can't make it through the day without your morning smoothie.
5. You sleep through earthquakes.
6. Your pastor has an agent.
7. You refuse to buy lotion without sunscreen.
8. Any temperature below 65 degrees is too cold for you.
9. You have more bottled water than food in your refrigerator.
10. At Starbucks, you see more people with laptops than with lattes.

About the Author

Nicole D. Sconiers is a screenwriter living in the sunny jungle of Los Angeles. She is also Editor of *Radio Facts* Magazine, a leading industry trade publication. The Hampton University grad co-founded It Is Written, a creative writing workshop for disadvantaged youth, and mentors young women in her spare time.

Glossary

Baby boy (adj.) a term of endearment for handsome men; interchangeable with honey dip, cutie pie.

Beat a face (vb.)—to apply makeup exceedingly well.

Big baller (adj.)—a man highly respected in the community for his ability to amass large sums of money, usually through questionable means. Interchangeable with Shot Caller, High Roller.

Clocking, to clock (vb.)—to imitate, usually accomplished through rigorous observation.

Cock blocking (vb., adv.)—originally used as a carnal expression to connote the interference of sexual intercourse; now used to describe persons interfering with any form of intercourse; "I was trying to get an interview with that soap opera hunk, but his agent was cock blocking!"

Crenshaw Cutie (adj.)—a black woman. Interchangeable with Rasheeda and Shaquita.

Dimepiece (adj.)—a measurement of cuteness; at the very top. Interchangeable with Hottie, Honey, Mommie, etc.

Dysfunctional Diva (n.)—the supreme queen of quirkiness.

Flossing (vb.)—to gaudily parade one's excessive material possessions; usually to the chagrin of the viewer.

Fly girl (adj.)—a woman known to wear the latest fashions, usually up-to-date on trends.

Ghettoism (n.)—a Standard English expression translated into Ebonics. For example "That's the way the cookie crumbles" becomes "It bees like that sometimes."

Glamazon (adj.)—a tall, beautiful woman, usually with a flair for fashion and a supermodel's attitude.

Grill (n.)—the face, usually used in a derogatory way.

Incognegro (adj.)—the art of reverse disguise; totally calling attention to oneself.

Kick down (vb.)—to provide with; usually through ill-begotten means

Left Coast (n.)—the coast opposite the Right one. La La Land.

Let them have it! (vb.)—to project an image of total perfection (usually emphasized with a finger snap).

Melrose Mommie (adj.)—a white woman. Interchangeable with Becky, Heidi, Barbie.

On and poppin' (vb.)—like a pan of grease. Let's get this party started!

Photo ops (adj.)—the opportunity to be photographed with a star, usually to the celebrity's disdain.

Pricetag tucker (adj.)—a woman who believes in the practice of buying clothes, tucking the pricetag out of sight, wearing the clothes, and then returning them to the store.
Also known as a Street Model.

Putting more on it (vb.)—exaggerating one's skills to impress others. "She claims she starred in Julia Roberts' last movie, but she was really putting more on it."

Rock (vb.)—to wear, usually done with flair.

Side gig (n.) a form of employment in addition to one's primary career, but usually held in more importance.

Street model (adj.)—see Pricetag Tucker.

To push up on (vb.)—to approach, usually a member of the opposite sex, in a quite intimate way.

To throw shade (vb.)—to hinder one's progress, usually through nefarious means.

Track addict (n.)—a person, particularly a woman, devoted to the practice of wearing weaves.

Twisted (vb.)—having an affection for a member of the same sex.

Weavologist (n.)—a person skilled in the art of sewing in fake hair; a track master.